A
HANDBOOK
OF
BASIC
DOCTRINES

A Compilation
of Scriptural
References

David K. Bernard

A Handbook of Basic Doctrines:
A Compilation of Scripture References
by David K. Bernard

©1988 David K. Bernard
Reprint History: 1990, 1991, 1993, 1995

Cover Design by Tim Agnew

All Scripture quotations in this book are from the King James Version of the Bible unless otherwise identified.

Printed in United States of America.

Printed by

LIBRARY OF CONGRESS
Library of Congress Cataloging-in-Publication Data

Bernard, David K., 1956-
    A handbook of basic doctrines : a compilation of scripture references / by David K. Bernard.
       p.   cm.
    ISBN 0-932581-37-4 :
    1. Oneness Pentecostal churches—Doctrines—Handbooks, manuals, etc. 2. Pentecostal churches—Doctrines—Handbooks, manuals, etc.
    I. Title.
BX8763.ZB47 1988
230′.994—dc19
                            88-19948
                              CIP

To
my son
Jonathan David
with love

TABLE OF CONTENTS

"Therefore leaving the principles of the doctrine of Christ, let us go on unto perfection; not laying again the foundation of repentance from dead works, and of faith toward God, of the doctrine of baptisms, and of laying on of hands, and of resurrection of the dead, and of eternal judgment" (Hebrews 6:1-2).

NOTE: An asterisk (*) denotes the most important scriptural references under a certain topic (in addition to the verses actually quoted).

Preface

"Search the scriptures" (John 5:39).

"They received the word with all readiness of mind, and searched the scriptures daily, whether those things were so" (Acts 17:11).

"The holy scriptures . . . are able to make thee wise unto salvation through faith which is in Christ Jesus. All scripture is given by inspiration of God, and is profitable for doctrine, for reproof, for correction, for instruction in righteousness: that the man of God may be perfect, throughly furnished unto all good works" (II Timothy 3:15-17).

There is great value in studying the Bible, the Word of God. The Bible reveals the way to salvation and eternal life. It is the final authority for faith and morals, doctrine and lifestyle. It is basically plain, meant to be understood, and meant to be read and obeyed by all.

This handbook has been prepared on the premise that the average person can, when shown the scriptural evidence itself, comprehend the basic teaching of the Bible. A book of this size cannot cover all important biblical truths, but this book does present the doctrines that, according to Hebrews 6:1-2, are foundational to Christian faith and life. Moreover, heeding the admonition of Hebrews 6:1 to "go on unto perfection," Part IV sets forth important aspects of practical Christian living.

The book has been designed for use as a reference work, for individual or group Bible study, and for witnessing. It can also be used to create color codes or chain references in a Bible. While the book seeks to be thorough, it does not try to be exhaustive. It does not necessarily list every Scripture reference that relates to a particular subject.

The most important Scripture verses under a certain topic are quoted, in whole or in part, or else their references are marked by an asterisk (*). These key verses are the most powerful texts under their respective headings and provide a summary of the biblical teaching on that subject. The unmarked Scripture references offer additional insight and support.

Due to limited scope and space, often only part of a relevant passage or verse has been reproduced. Moreover, no attempt has been made to exegete or explain the verses of Scripture cited. The reader should be careful to ascertain the total context of each verse and to use proper rules of biblical interpretation in seeking to understand the verse. To see how the author interprets and applies a certain verse, or to see why a verse is included under a particular topic, the reader is referred to the author's *Series in Pentecostal Theology,* which consists of four volumes: *The Oneness of God, The New Birth, In Search of Holiness,* and *Practical Holiness: A Second Look.* These books discuss in greater detail most of the topics and Scripture references listed in this handbook.

I
GOD

"The principles of the doctrine of Christ, . . . the foundation . . . of faith toward God" (Hebrews 6:1).

A. God is One

"Hear, O Israel: the LORD our God is one LORD" (Deuteronomy 6:4).

"O LORD of hosts, God of Israel, that dwellest between the cherubims, thou art the God, even thou alone, of all the kingdoms of the earth: thou hast made heaven and earth" (Isaiah 37:16).

"Thus saith the LORD the King of Israel, and his redeemer the LORD of hosts; I am the first, and I am the last; and beside me there is no God. . . . Is there a God beside me? yea, there is no God; I know not any. . . . Thus saith the LORD, thy redeemer, and he that formed thee from the womb, I am the LORD that maketh all things; that stretcheth forth the heavens alone; that spreadeth abroad the earth by myself" (Isaiah 44:6, 8, 24).

"I am the LORD, and there is none else, there is no God beside me. . . . That they may know from the rising of the sun, and from the west, that there is none beside me. I am the LORD, and there is none else. . . . For thus saith the LORD that created the heavens; God himself that formed the earth and made it . . . I am the LORD; and there is none else. . . . There is no God else beside me; a just God and a Saviour; there is none beside me. Look unto me, and be ye saved, all the ends of the earth; for I am God, and there is none else" (Isaiah 45:5-6, 18, 21-22).

"To whom will ye liken me, and make me equal, and compare me that we may be like? . . . I am God, and there is none else; I am God, and there is none like me" (Isaiah 46:5, 9).

"I will not give my glory unto another. . . . I am he; I am the first, I also am the last" (Isaiah 48:11-12).

"And Jesus answered him, The first of all the commandments is, Hear, O Israel; The Lord our God is one Lord" (Mark 12:29).

"God is one" (Galatians 3:20).

"For there is one God, and one mediator between God and men, the man Christ Jesus" (I Timothy 2:5).

"Thou believest that there is one God; thou doest well: the devils also believe, and tremble" (James 2:19).

12

"A throne was set in heaven, and one sat on the throne" (Revelation 4:2).

Exodus 20:3-5	* Isaiah 42:8
Deuteronomy 4:35	* Isaiah 43:10-11
Deuteronomy 5:7	* Isaiah 45:5-6, 14, 18,
Deuteronomy 32:39	21-22
II Samuel 7:22	Hosea 13:4
I Kings 8:60	* Zechariah 14:9
I Chronicles 17:20	* Malachi 2:10
Nehemiah 9:6	John 4:22-24
Job 9:8	* John 17:3
Psalm 71:22	* Romans 3:30
Psalm 83:18	I Corinthians 8:4, 6
Psalm 86:10	Ephesians 4:6
Isaiah 1:4; 5:19, etc.	I Timothy 6:15
Isaiah 40:25	I John 2:20

B. God is an Invisible Spirit

"No man hath seen God at any time" (John 1:18).

"God is a Spirit" (John 4:24).

Exodus 33:20	* I Timothy 6:15-16
Matthew 16:17	Hebrews 11:27
Luke 24:39	Hebrews 12:9
Colossians 1:15	I John 4:12
I Timothy 1:17	

C. Father, Son, and Holy Ghost
1. The Father—God in Parental Relationship

"Is not he thy father that hath bought thee? hath he not made thee, and established thee?" (Deuteronomy 32:6).

"Thou, O LORD, art our father, our redeemer" (Isaiah 63:16).

"Have we not all one father? hath not one God created us?" (Malachi 2:10).

Psalm 89:26   Galatians 1:1-4
Isaiah 64:8   Ephesians 4:6
Jeremiah 31:9   Hebrews 12:9
Romans 8:14-16

2. The Son of God (Humanity)

"And the angel answered and said unto her, The Holy Ghost shall come upon thee, and the power of the Highest shall overshadow thee: therefore also that holy thing which shall be born of thee shall be called the Son of God" (Luke 1:35).

"We were reconciled to God by the death of his Son" (Romans 5:10).

"But when the fulness of the time was come, God

14

sent forth his Son, made of a woman, made under the law'' (Galatians 4:4).

"God . . . hath in these last days spoken unto us by his Son . . . who being the brightness of his glory, and the express image of his person . . ." (Hebrews 1:1-3).

"Thou art my Son, this day have I begotten thee. . . . I will be to him a Father, and he shall be to me a Son" (Hebrews 1:5).

Psalm 2:7	John 14:10-11, 28
Isaiah 7:14	Acts 13:33
* Isaiah 9:6	I Corinthians 15:23-28
* Matthew 1:18-23	* Colossians 1:13-15
Mark 13:32	* Hebrews 1:1-9
John 5:17-19	Hebrews 7:28
John 8:42	

3. The Holy Spirit—God in Activity as Spirit

"And the Spirit of God moved upon the face of the waters" (Genesis 1:2).

"Why hath Satan filled thine heart to lie to the Holy Ghost? . . . Thou hast not lied unto men, but unto God. . . . How is it that ye have agreed together to tempt the Spirit of the Lord?" (Acts 5:3, 4, 9).

"There is one body, and one Spirit . . . one God and

15

Father of all, who is above all, and through all, and in you all'' (Ephesians 4:4, 6).

Leviticus 11:44	I Corinthians 12:11
John 4:24	I Peter 1:16
I Corinthians 3:16;	II Peter 1:21
6:19	

4. The Father is the Holy Ghost

"She was found with child of the Holy Ghost. . . . For that which is conceived in her is of the Holy Ghost'' (Matthew 1:18, 20).

"For it is not ye that speak, but the Spirit of your Father which speaketh in you'' (Matthew 10:20).

Genesis 1:2	* Luke 1:35
Isaiah 40:13	Romans 8:15-16
Joel 2:27-28	Ephesians 3:14-16

Matthew 10:20 and Mark 13:11
John 14:17 and 14:23
John 14:26 and II Corinthians 1:3-4
I Corinthians 3:16-17 and 6:19
* Ephesians 1:17-20 and Romans 8:11
I Timothy 6:13 and Romans 8:11
II Timothy 3:16 and II Peter 1:21
* I Peter 1:2 and Jude 1

D. The Deity of Jesus Christ
1. Jesus is God Incarnate

"For unto us a child is born, unto us a son is given: and the government shall be upon his shoulder: and his name shall be called Wonderful, Counsellor, The mighty God, The everlasting Father, The Prince of Peace" (Isaiah 9:6).

"Behold your God" (Isaiah 40:9).

"In the beginning was the Word, and the Word was with God, and the Word was God. . . . And the Word was made flesh" (John 1:1, 14).

"My Lord and my God" (John 20:28).

"God was in Christ, reconciling the world unto himself" (II Corinthians 5:19).

"Who is the image of the invisible God" (Colossians 1:15).

"For in him dwelleth all the fulness of the Godhead bodily. And ye are complete in him, which is the head of all principality and power" (Colossians 2:9-10).

"God was manifest in the flesh" (I Timothy 3:16).

"The great God and our Savior Jesus Christ" (Titus 2:13).

Isaiah 7:14
Isaiah 11:1, 10
Isaiah 40:3
* Micah 5:2
Zechariah 12:8
* Matthew 1:23
Matthew 26:63-65
* John 1:1-18
John 5:18
John 10:33
Acts 20:28
Romans 9:5
II Corinthians 4:4
Ephesians 5:5

* Colossians 1:19
Colossians 2:2
II Thessalonians 1:12
I Timothy 5:21
II Timothy 4:1
II Peter 1:1
* Hebrews 1:1-3
Hebrews 3:5-6
* I John 5:20
* Jude 4, 25
* Revelation 1:7-18;
4:1-11
* Revelation 22:3-4

* Exodus 20:1-5 and Luke 24:52
Deuteronomy 33:27 and Revelation 1:8, 18
Psalm 139:1-6 and John 21:17
Psalm 139:7-13 and Matthew 18:20; 28:20
* Isaiah 35:3-6 and Matthew 11:2-6
Isaiah 40:3 and Matthew 3:3
* Isaiah 43:25 and Mark 2:5-12
Ecclesiastes 12:7 and Acts 7:59
Malachi 3:6 and Hebrews 13:8
Hebrews 11:10 and John 14:3
I John 1:5 and John 1:4-9
Ephesians 2:4 and 5:25
Revelation 19:6 and Colossians 1:16-18

2. From the Beginning of His Human Life

"But thou, Bethlehem . . . out of thee shall he come forth unto me that is to be ruler in Israel; whose goings forth have been from of old, from everlasting" (Micah 5:2).

"Behold, a virgin shall be with child, and shall bring forth a son, and they shall call his name Emmanuel, which being interpreted is, God with us" (Matthew 1:23).

Isaiah 7:14	Luke 2:26
Isaiah 9:6	Luke 2:38
Matthew 2:11	Hebrews 1:6
* Luke 1:35	

3. The Divine Nature of Jesus is the Father

"For unto us a child is born, unto us a son is given . . . and his name shall be called Wonderful, Counsellor, The mighty God, The everlasting Father, The Prince of Peace" (Isaiah 9:6).

"Thou, O LORD, art our father, our redeemer" (Isaiah 63:16).

"I and my Father are one" (John 10:30).

"Philip saith unto him, Lord, shew us the Father, and it sufficeth us. Jesus saith unto him, Have I been so long time with you, and yet hast thou not known

19

me, Philip? he that hath seen me hath seen the Father; and how sayest thou then, Shew us the Father? Believest thou not that I am in the Father, and the Father in me? the words that I speak unto you I speak not of myself: but the Father that dwelleth in me, he doeth the works. Believe me that I am in the Father, and the Father in me: or else believe me for the very works' sake" (John 14:8-11).

"I am Alpha and Omega, the beginning and the end. I will give unto him that is athirst of the fountain of the water of life freely. He that overcometh shall inherit all things: and I will be his God, and he shall be my son" (Revelation 21:6-7).

John 8:19-27   John 14:18
John 10:38   * Colossians 2:9
John 12:45   I John 3:1-5

*   John 2:19-21 and Acts 2:24
    John 6:40 and I Corinthians 6:14
    John 6:44 and John 12:32
    John 14:14 and John 16:23
    John 16:7 and John 14:26
    Ephesians 5:26 and Jude 1

4. The Divine Nature of Jesus is the Holy Spirit

"And I will pray the Father, and he shall give you another Comforter, that he may abide with you for ever: even the Spirit of truth; whom the world cannot receive, because it seeth him not, neither knoweth him: but ye know him; for he dwelleth with you, and shall be in you. I will not leave you comfortless: I will come to you" (John 14:16-18).

"Now the Lord is that Spirit: and where the Spirit of the Lord is, there is liberty" (II Corinthians 3:17).

John 16:7   Ephesians 3:16-17
Acts 16:6-7 (NIV)   * Philippians 1:19
* Galatians 4:6

Matthew 28:20 and John 14:16
* Luke 21:15 and Mark 13:11
* John 2:19-21 and Romans 8:9-11
   John 6:40 and Romans 8:11
   Ephesians 5:26 and I Peter 1:2
* Colossians 1:27 and Acts 2:4, 38
   Hebrews 7:25 and Romans 8:26
   I Peter 1:10-11 and II Peter 1:21
   I John 2:1 and John 14:26

5. Jesus is Jehovah (the LORD in the KJV)

"Behold, the days come, saith the LORD, that I will raise unto David a righteous Branch, and a King shall reign and prosper, and shall execute judgment and justice in the earth. In his days Judah shall be saved, and Israel shall dwell safely: and this is his name whereby he shall be called, THE LORD OUR RIGHT-EOUSNESS" (Jeremiah 23:5-6).

21

"Thus saith the LORD my God. . . . So they weighed for my price thirty pieces of silver" (Zechariah 11:4, 12).

"The burden of the word of the LORD for Israel, saith the LORD. . . . They shall look upon me whom they have pierced" (Zechariah 12:1, 10).

"Before Abraham was, I am" (John 8:58).

"And he said, Who art thou, Lord? And the Lord said, I am Jesus" (Acts 9:5).

Isaiah 40:10   Jeremiah 33:15-16
Isaiah 52:6   *   Zechariah 14:3-5
Isaiah 53:1-2   Malachi 3:1
Isaiah 59:16   Revelation 22:6, 16

Genesis 17:1 and Revelation 1:8, 18
*   Exodus 3:14 and John 8:56-59
Exodus 15:26 and James 5:14-15
Exodus 31:13 and Ephesians 5:26
Exodus 34:14 and Luke 24:52
Judges 6:24 and John 14:27
I Samuel 1:3 and James 5:4-7
Psalm 7:17 and Luke 1:76, 78
Psalm 18:2 and I Corinthians 10:4
Psalm 18:2 and Luke 1:69
Psalm 23:1 and John 10:11
Psalm 24:7-10 and I Corinthians 2:8
Psalm 27:1 and John 8:12

Psalm 27:1 and Acts 4:10-12
Psalm 68:18 and Ephesians 4:7-10
* Psalm 136:3 and Revelation 19:16
Isaiah 12:6 and Acts 2:27
Isaiah 33:22 and Hebrews 9:14-17
Isaiah 33:22 and Acts 10:42
* Isaiah 40:3 and Matthew 3:3
* Isaiah 40:5 and I Corinthians 2:8
    (see also Isaiah 42:8; 48:11)
Isaiah 41:4 and Revelation 1:8, 18
Isaiah 43:11 and Titus 2:13
Isaiah 44:3 and John 7:38-39
Isaiah 44:6 and John 1:49
Isaiah 44:24 and John 1:3
Isaiah 45:21 and Acts 7:52
* Isaiah 45:23 and Philippians 2:10
Isaiah 54:5 and Galatians 3:13

E. The Name of Jesus (Jehovah-Savior)
1. Supreme Revelation of God in the New Testament

"Therefore my people shall know my name: therefore they shall know in that day that I am he that doth speak: behold, it is I" (Isaiah 52:6).

"And the LORD shall be king over all the earth: in that day shall there be one LORD, and his name one" (Zechariah 14:9).

"And whatsoever ye shall ask in my name, that will I do, that the Father may be glorified in the Son. If ye shall ask any thing in my name, I will do it" (John 14:13-14).

"In the name of Jesus Christ of Nazareth rise up and walk. . . . And his name through faith in his name hath made this man strong" (Acts 3:6, 16).

"Wherefore God also hath highly exalted him, and given him a name which is above every name: that at the name of Jesus every knee should bow, of things in heaven, and things in earth, and things under the earth; and that every tongue should confess that Jesus Christ is Lord, to the glory of God the Father" (Philippians 2:9-11).

"And whatsoever ye do in word or deed, do all in the name of the Lord Jesus, giving thanks to God and the Father by him" (Colossians 3:17).

Matthew 10:22	Acts 5:28, 41
Matthew 18:20	Acts 9:21
Mark 16:17-18	Acts 15:26
John 5:43	Acts 16:18
John 14:26	Acts 19:13-17
John 17:6, 26	Ephesians 3:14-15
* Acts 4:7-12	Hebrews 1:4
* Acts 4:17-18, 30	Hebrews 2:12
	James 5:14

2. The Saving Name

"And she shall bring forth a son, and thou shalt call his name JESUS: for he shall save his people from their sins" (Matthew 1:21).

"Neither is there salvation in any other: for there is none other name under heaven given among men, whereby we must be saved" (Acts 4:12).

"Through his name whosoever believeth in him shall receive remission of sins" (Acts 10:43).

---

* Luke 24:47
  Acts 2:21
  Acts 3:16
  Acts 15:14-17

  Acts 22:16
  Romans 10:13
  I John 2:12

II
SALVATION

"The foundation of repentance from dead works, and of faith toward God, of the doctrine of baptisms . . ." (Hebrews 6:1-2).

A. Universal Need for Salvation

"We have before proved both Jews and Gentiles, that they are all under sin; as it is written, There is none righteous, no, not one: there is none that understandeth, there is none that seeketh after God. They are all gone out of the way, they are together become unprofitable; there is none that doeth good, no, not one" (Romans 3:9-12).

"For all have sinned, and come short of the glory of God" (Romans 3:23).

"By one man sin entered into the world, and death by sin; and so death passed upon all men, for that all have sinned. . . . By one man's disobedience many were made sinners" (Romans 5:12, 19).

27

"For the wages of sin is death" (Romans 6:23).

I Kings 8:46	Jeremiah 17:9
II Chronicles 6:30	Romans 2:12-16
Psalm 14:1-3	Romans 3:19
Psalm 53:1-3	* Galatians 3:22
Psalm 130:3	* Ephesians 2:1-3
Proverbs 20:9	James 1:15
Ecclesiastes 7:20	* I John 1:8-10
Isaiah 53:6	I John 5:19
Isaiah 64:6	

B. The Atoning Work of Jesus Christ

"He was wounded for our transgressions, he was bruised for our iniquities: the chastisement of our peace was upon him; and with his stripes we are healed. . . . The LORD hath laid on him the iniquity of us all" (Isaiah 53:5-6).

"For this is my blood of the new testament, which is shed for many for the remission of sins" (Matthew 26:28).

"Behold the Lamb of God, which taketh away the sin of the world" (John 1:29).

"Being justified freely by his grace through the redemption that is in Christ Jesus: whom God hath set forth to be a propitiation through faith in his blood" (Romans 3:24-25).

28

"God commendeth his love toward us, in that, while we were yet sinners, Christ died for us. Much more then, being now justified by his blood, we shall be saved from wrath through him. For if, when we were enemies, we were reconciled to God by the death of his Son, much more, being reconciled, we shall be saved by his life. And not only so, but we also joy in God through our Lord Jesus Christ, by whom we have now received the atonement" (Romans 5:8-11).

"For there is one God, and one mediator between God and men, the man Christ Jesus; who gave himself a ransom for all" (I Timothy 2:5-6).

"That he by the grace of God should taste death for every man" (Hebrews 2:9).

Exodus 12:13	* Ephesians 2:13-19
Leviticus 25:25, 47-49	Ephesians 5:25-27
Matthew 20:28	* Colossians 1:19-22
John 8:24	* Colossians 2:13-15
John 14:6	* Hebrews 9:22, 28
Romans 4:24-25	* Hebrews 10:4
Romans 5:15-21	* Hebrews 10:10-20
I Corinthians 5:7	I Peter 1:18-20
* I Corinthians 15:1-4	I Peter 2:24
* II Corinthians 5:14-21	I John 2:2
Galatians 3:13-14	Revelation 5:8-10

C. Salvation is by Grace

"Being justified freely by his grace" (Romans 3:24).

"For by grace are ye saved through faith; and that not of yourselves: it is the gift of God: not of works, lest any man should boast. For we are his workmanship, created in Christ Jesus unto good works, which God hath before ordained that we should walk in them" (Ephesians 2:8-10).

"For it is God which worketh in you both to will and to do of his good pleasure" (Philippians 2:13).

"For the grace of God that bringeth salvation hath appeared to all men, teaching us that, denying ungodliness and worldly lusts, we should live soberly, righteously, and godly, in this present world" (Titus 2:11-12).

Genesis 6:8
Psalm 84:11
Acts 15:7-11
Romans 4:4, 16
Romans 5:20
* Romans 6:1-2, 15, 23
Romans 8:32
I Corinthians 10:13
I Corinthians 15:10
II Corinthians 9:8-9

* II Corinthians 12:9
Galatians 5:4
* Ephesians 2:4-10
* Titus 3:4-7
Hebrews 4:16
Hebrews 12:15
James 1:17
* James 4:6
I Peter 5:5, 10

D. Salvation is through Faith
1. Only Through Faith in Jesus Christ

"For God so loved the world, that he gave his only begotten Son, that whosoever believeth in him should not perish, but have everlasting life" (John 3:16).

"If ye believe not that I am he, ye shall die in your sins" (John 8:24).

"But these are written, that ye might believe that Jesus is the Christ, the Son of God; and that believing ye might have life through his name" (John 20:31).

"Believe on the Lord Jesus Christ, and thou shalt be saved" (Acts 16:31).

"For I am not ashamed of the gospel of Christ: for it is the power of God unto salvation to every one that believeth. . . . For therein is the righteousness of God revealed from faith to faith: as it is written, The just shall live by faith" (Romans 1:16-17).

"Knowing that a man is not justified by the works of the law, but by the faith of Jesus Christ, even we have believed in Jesus Christ, that we might be justified by the faith of Christ, and not by the works of the law: for by the works of the law shall no flesh be justified." (Galatians 2:16).

"For by grace are ye saved through faith" (Ephesians 2:8).

"But without faith it is impossible to please him: for he that cometh to God must believe that he is, and that he is a rewarder of them that diligently seek him" (Hebrews 11:6).

Habakkuk 2:4   Romans 4:1-25
John 1:12   * Romans 10:8-11
John 3:17-18   Galatians 2:20
John 3:36   Galatians 3:1-11
John 6:47   Galatians 3:22-25
John 14:6   Hebrews 10:38
Acts 13:38-39   Hebrews 11:7
Acts 15:7-11   I John 5:1-13
* Romans 3:21-31

2. Saving Faith Includes Obedience

"A great company of the priests were obedient to the faith" (Acts 6:7).

"By whom we have received grace and apostleship, for obedience to the faith among all nations, for his name" (Romans 1:5).

"Ye were the servants of sin, but ye have obeyed from the heart that form of doctrine" (Romans 6:17).

"But they have not all obeyed the gospel. For Esaias saith, Lord, who hath believed our report?" (Romans 10:16).

"Made known to all nations for the obedience of faith" (Romans 16:26).

"In flaming fire taking vengeance on them that know not God, and that obey not the gospel of our Lord Jesus Christ" (II Thessalonians 1:8).

"He became the author of eternal salvation unto all them that obey him" (Hebrews 5:9).

Matthew 7:21	* Hebrews 11:28
* John 8:30-32	* James 1:21-25
John 14:15, 23	* I Peter 1:21-23
Acts 5:32	I Peter 4:17
Romans 15:18	* I John 2:3-6
* II Thessalonians 1:7-10	* I John 5:1-8
* Hebrews 11:6-10	

Romans 4:3 and Genesis 15:6; 22:16-18; 26:5
Romans 10:6-10 and Deuteronomy 30:10-14; Luke 6:46

3. Examples of Insufficient, Mental Faith

"Many believed in his name, when they saw the miracles which he did. But Jesus did not commit himself unto them, . . . for he knew what was in man" (John 2:23-25).

"Among the chief rulers also many believed on him; but because of the Pharisees they did not confess him, lest they should be put out of the synagogue: for they loved the praise of men more than the praise of God" (John 12:42-43).

"Thou believest that there is one God; thou doest well: the devils also believe, and tremble" (James 2:19).

---

* Matthew 7:13-27   Luke 13:23-30
  Matthew 8:29   *Acts 8:12-23
  Luke 8:11-15   James 2:14-26

4. Saving Faith Includes the Acts 2:38 Experience

"Repent ye, and believe the gospel" (Mark 1:15).

"He that believeth and is baptized shall be saved" (Mark 16:16).

"He that believeth on me, as the scripture hath said, out of his belly shall flow rivers of living water. (But this spake he of the Spirit, which they that believe on him should receive: for the Holy Ghost was not yet given; because that Jesus was not yet glorified.)" (John 7:38-39).

"The Holy Ghost fell on them, as on us at the beginning. . . . God gave them the like gift as he did unto us, who believed on the Lord Jesus Christ" (Acts 11:15, 17).

"Have ye received the Holy Ghost since ye believed? . . . Unto what then were ye baptized?" (Acts 19:2-3).

"That the blessing of Abraham might come on the Gentiles through Jesus Christ; that we might receive the promise of the Spirit through faith" (Galatians 3:14).

"In whom ye also trusted, after that ye heard the word of truth, the gospel of your salvation: in whom also after that ye believed, ye were sealed with that holy Spirit of promise" (Ephesians 1:13).

Luke 13:3	Acts 18:8
Acts 2:41	*Acts 19:1-6
Acts 8:12	Galatians 3:2
Acts 8:36-39	I John 5:8-10
Acts 16:30-34	

Romans 10:8-13 with Luke 6:46; Acts 2:4, 21; 22:16; Romans 8:9-11; and I Corinthians 12:3

E. Obeying (Applying) the Gospel
1. New Testament Teaching

"I indeed baptize you with water unto repentance: but he that cometh after me is mightier than I, whose shoes I am not worthy to bear: he shall baptize you with the Holy Ghost, and with fire" (Matthew 3:11).

"Except a man be born of water and of the Spirit,

he cannot enter into the kingdom of God" (John 3:5).

"Repent, and be baptized every one of you in the name of Jesus Christ for the remission of sins, and ye shall receive the gift of the Holy Ghost" (Acts 2:38).

"How shall we, that are dead to sin, live any longer therein? . . . We are buried with him by baptism into death: that like as Christ was raised up from the dead by the glory of the Father, even so we also should walk in newness of life. . . . For the law of the Spirit of life in Christ Jesus hath made me free from the law of sin and death" (Romans 6:2, 4; 8:2).

"But ye are washed, but ye are sanctified, but ye are justified in the name of the Lord Jesus, and by the Spirit of our God" (I Corinthians 6:11).

"I declare unto you the gospel which I preached unto you, which also ye have received, and wherein ye stand; by which also ye are saved, if ye keep in memory what I preached unto you, unless ye have believed in vain. For I delivered unto you first of all that which I also received, how that Christ died for our sins according to the scriptures; and that he was buried, and that he rose again the third day according to the scriptures" (I Corinthians 15:1-4).

"Not by works of righteousness which we have done, but according to his mercy he saved us, by the washing of regeneration, and renewing of the Holy Ghost" (Titus 3:5).

"And there are three that bear witness in earth, the Spirit, and the water, and the blood: and these three agree in one" (I John 5:8).

Mark 1:8	* Acts 10:43-48
Mark 16:15-17	Acts 11:15-18
Luke 3:16	Acts 16:30-34
Luke 24:46-49	* Acts 19:1-6
Acts 1:4-8	* Romans 6:1-7; 7:6; 8:2
Acts 3:19	I Corinthians 10:1-2
* Acts 8:15-17	Hebrews 6:1-2
Acts 8:36-39	Hebrews 10:15-23
* Acts 9:17-18; 22:16	* I John 5:8-10

2. Old Testament Typology (Blood, Water, Fire or Oil)

"Our fathers were under the cloud, and all passed through the sea; and were all baptized unto Moses in the cloud and in the sea" (I Corinthians 10:1-2).

---

* Exodus 12:13; 14:19-31	Numbers 19:1-10
* Exodus 19:10-11	Numbers 31:1-18
* Exodus 29:1-7	Numbers 31:21-24
Leviticus 1:1-13	I Kings 18:33-39
Leviticus 14:1-20	Hebrews 9:18-20

* Exodus 40:6-7 and Hebrews 9:1-9
  Matthew 3:11 and Acts 2:3-4
  John 14:16-17, 26 and I John 2:20, 27

I Peter 3:20-21 and II Peter 3:5-7

F. Repentance
1. Necessity of Repentance

"Except ye repent, ye shall all likewise perish" (Luke 13:3, 5).

"Repent . . ." (Acts 2:38).

"Repent ye therefore, and be converted, that your sins may be blotted out, when the times of refreshing shall come from the presence of the Lord" (Acts 3:19).

"And the times of this ignorance God winked at; but now commandeth all men every where to repent" (Acts 17:30).

Ezekiel 18:30-32	Luke 24:47
Ezekiel 33:11	Acts 26:18, 20
Matthew 3:1-11	Romans 2:4
Matthew 4:17	* Hebrews 6:1
Mark 1:4-5	II Peter 3:9
* Mark 1:15	Revelation 2:5
Mark 6:12	Revelation 2:16
Luke 3:3-9	Revelation 2:21-22
* Luke 13:1-5	Revelation 3:3

2. Elements of Repentance

"The sacrifices of God are a broken spirit: a broken and a contrite heart, O God, thou wilt not despise" (Psalm 51:17).

38

"He that covereth his sins shall not prosper: but whoso confesseth and forsaketh them shall have mercy" (Proverbs 28:13).

"Bring forth therefore fruits worthy of repentance" (Luke 3:8).

"To open their eyes, and to turn them from darkness to light, and from the power of Satan unto God, that they may receive forgiveness of sins, and inheritance among them which are sanctified by faith. . . . That they should repent and turn to God, and do works meet for repentance" (Acts 26:18, 20).

"For godly sorrow worketh repentance to salvation not to be repented of: but the sorrow of the world worketh death" (II Corinthians 7:10).

Psalm 51:1-12   Luke 15:11-32
Matthew 5:3   Luke 18:9-14
Matthew 5:23-24   Luke 19:8
* Mark 1:4-5   Acts 19:18-19
Mark 2:17   Hebrews 6:1
* Luke 3:7-9   I John 1:9
Luke 5:32

G. Water Baptism
1. Significance and Necessity

"He that believeth and is baptized shall be saved" (Mark 16:16).

"Except a man be born of water and of the Spirit, he cannot enter into the kingdom of God" (John 3:5).

"Repent, and be baptized every one of you in the name of Jesus Christ for the remission of sins . . ." (Acts 2:38).

"And he commanded them to be baptized in the name of the Lord" (Acts 10:48).

"And now why tarriest thou? arise, and be baptized, and wash away thy sins, calling on the name of the Lord" (Acts 22:16).

"Know ye not, that so many of us as were baptized into Jesus Christ were baptized into his death? Therefore we are buried with him by baptism into death" (Romans 6:3-4).

"But ye are washed, but ye are sanctified, but ye are justified in the name of the Lord Jesus, and by the Spirit of our God" (I Corinthians 6:11).

"For as many of you as have been baptized into Christ have put on Christ" (Galatians 3:27).

"In whom also ye are circumcised with the circumcision made without hands, in putting off the body of the sins of the flesh by the circumcision of Christ: buried with him in baptism . . ." (Colossians 2:11-12).

"The like figure whereunto even baptism doth also

now save us" (I Peter 3:20-21).

Exodus 30:20

Leviticus 14:1-7

Leviticus 17:15-16

Numbers 19:1-5, 9

Numbers 19:13, 20

II Kings 5:10-14

Matthew 3:11

Matthew 28:19

Mark 1:4

Luke 3:3

Luke 7:30

Luke 24:47

John 20:23

* Colossians 2:11-13

* Titus 3:5

Hebrews 9:19

* I Peter 3:20-21

* I John 5:6, 8

2. For Repentant Believers

"Then said he to the multitude that came forth to be baptized of him . . . Bring forth therefore fruits worthy of repentance" (Luke 3:7-8).

"Repent, and be baptized every one of you . . ." (Acts 2:38).

"Then they that gladly received his word were baptized" (Acts 2:41).

"But when they believed Philip preaching the things concerning the kingdom of God, and the name of Jesus Christ, they were baptized, both men and women" (Acts 8:12).

"The eunuch said, See, here is water; what doth hinder me to be baptized? And Philip said, If thou believest with all thine heart thou mayest" (Acts 8:36-37).

"Many of the Corinthians hearing believed, and were baptized" (Acts 18:8).

---

* Matthew 3:6-8	Acts 10:47-48
Mark 1:5	Acts 16:14-15
* Mark 16:16	Acts 16:31-34
Acts 9:6, 18	* Acts 19:5
Acts 10:43	Hebrews 11:6

3. The Baptismal Mode: Immersion in Water

"And Jesus, when he was baptized, went up straightway out of the water" (Matthew 3:16).

"And John also was baptizing in Aenon near to Salim because there was much water there" (John 3:23).

"And as they went on their way, they came unto a certain water: and the eunuch said, See, here is water; what doth hinder me to be baptized? . . . And they went down both into the water, both Philip and the eunuch; and he baptized him. And when they were come up out of the water, the Spirit of the Lord caught away Philip" (Acts 8:36-39).

"We are buried with him by baptism" (Romans 6:4).

"Buried with him in baptism" (Colossians 2:12).

Matthew 15:6   Mark 7:8
* Mark 1:5   Acts 10:47-48
* Mark 1:9-10

4. The Baptismal Formula: In the Name of Jesus

"Be baptized every one of you in the name of Jesus Christ" (Acts 2:38).

"They were baptized in the name of the Lord Jesus" (Acts 8:16).

"And he commanded them to be baptized in the name of the Lord" (Acts 10:48). [Earliest Greek texts say, "in the name of Jesus Christ."]

"And he said unto them, Unto what then were ye baptized? And they said, Unto John's baptism. Then said Paul, John verily baptized with the baptism of repentance, saying unto the people, that they should believe on him which should come after him, that is, on Christ Jesus. When they heard this, they were baptized in the name of the Lord Jesus" (Acts 19:3-5).

"Arise, and be baptized, and wash away thy sins, calling on the name of the Lord" (Acts 22:16). [Earliest Greek texts say, "on his name."]

John 14:6-14
Acts 3:6, 16
Acts 4:7-12
* Acts 8:12
Acts 10:43
* Acts 15:17
Romans 6:3
Romans 6:4
* I Corinthians 1:13

I Corinthians 6:11
Galatians 3:27
Ephesians 3:14-15
Philippians 2:9-11
Colossians 2:9-10
Colossians 2:12
* Colossians 3:17
* James 2:7

5. The One Name in Matthew 28:19

"All power is given unto me in heaven and in earth. Go ye therefore, and teach all nations, baptizing them in the name of the Father, and of the Son, and of the Holy Ghost: teaching them to observe all things whatsoever I have commanded you: and, lo, I am with you alway, even unto the end of the world" (Matthew 28:18-20).

"In that day shall there be one LORD, and his name one" (Zechariah 14:9).

"And she shall bring forth a son, and thou shalt call his name JESUS" (Matthew 1:21).

"And that repentance and remission of sins should be preached in his name among all nations, beginning at Jerusalem" (Luke 24:47).

"I am come in my Father's name" (John 5:43).

"But the Comforter, which is the Holy Ghost, whom the Father will send in my name . . ." (John 14:26).

"And there shall be no more curse: but the throne of God and of the Lamb shall be in it; and his servants shall serve him: and they shall see his face; and his name shall be in their foreheads" (Revelation 22:3-4).

Psalm 22:22   * Acts 19:3-5
Isaiah 9:6   Philippians 2:9-11
* Isaiah 52:6   Colossians 3:17
Mark 16:15-17   Hebrews 1:4
John 17:6, 26   Hebrews 2:12
* Acts 2:38; 8:16; 10:48

H. The Baptism of the Holy Ghost
1. Promise and Command

"And it shall come to pass afterward, that I will pour out my spirit upon all flesh; and your sons and your daughters shall prophesy, your old men shall dream dreams, your young men shall see visions; and also upon the servants and upon the handmaids in those days will I pour out my spirit" (Joel 2:28-29).

"He shall baptize you with the Holy Ghost, and with fire" (Matthew 3:11).

"Receive ye the Holy Ghost" (John 20:22).

"And, being assembled together with them, commanded them that they should not depart from Jerusalem, but wait for the promise of the Father, which, saith he, ye have heard of me. For John truly baptized with water; but ye shall be baptized with the Holy Ghost not many days hence" (Acts 1:4-5).

"And ye shall receive the gift of the Holy Ghost. For the promise is unto you, and to your children, and to all that are afar off, even as many as the Lord our God shall call" (Acts 2:38-39).

———

Jeremiah 31:31-33
Ezekiel 11:19
Ezekiel 36:26
Ezekiel 39:29
Matthew 28:20
Mark 1:8
Mark 15:17-18
Luke 3:16
* Luke 11:13
* Luke 24:49
John 1:33
* John 3:5

John 4:14
* John 7:38-39
* John 14:16-18
John 14:26
John 15:26
* John 16:7, 13
* Acts 1:4-8
Acts 2:16-18
II Corinthians 3:3-6
Hebrews 10:15-16
I Peter 1:10-12

2. An Experience for the Church Founded on Pentecost

"Upon this rock I will build my church" (Matthew 16:18).

"Among those that are born of women there is not a greater prophet than John the Baptist: but he that is least in the kingdom of God is greater than he" (Luke 7:28).

"And that repentance and remission of sins should be preached in his name among all nations, beginning at Jerusalem. . . . And behold, I send the promise of my Father upon you: but tarry ye in the city of Jerusalem, until ye be endued with power from on high" (Luke 24:47, 49).

"For the Holy Ghost was not yet given; because that Jesus was not yet glorified" (John 7:39).

"If I go not away, the Comforter will not come unto you; but if I depart, I will send him unto you" (John 16:7).

"Ye shall be baptized with the Holy Ghost not many days hence" (Acts 1:5).

"But when the fulness of the time was come, God sent forth his Son, made of a woman, made under the law, to redeem them that were under the law, that we might receive the adoption of sons. And because ye are sons, God hath sent forth the Spirit of his Son into your hearts, crying, Abba, Father" (Galatians 4:4-6).

Jeremiah 31:31-33   Matthew 3:11
Ezekiel 11:19   Luke 3:16

John 1:16-17	Romans 8:3-4
* Acts 1:4-8	Galatians 3:13-14
* Acts 2:1-4	* Hebrews 8:6-13
Acts 2:33	* Hebrews 9:15-17
Acts 19:1-6	* Hebrews 11:39-40
Romans 4:24-25	* I Peter 1:10-12

3. Significance and Necessity

"Except a man be born of water and of the Spirit, he cannot enter into the kingdom of God" (John 3:5).

"But ye shall receive power, after that the Holy Ghost is come upon you: and ye shall be witnesses unto me" (Acts 1:8).

"But ye are not in the flesh, but in the Spirit, if so be that the Spirit of God dwell in you. Now if any man have not the Spirit of Christ, he is none of his" (Romans 8:9).

"For the kingdom of God is . . . righteousness, and peace, and joy in the Holy Ghost" (Romans 14:17).

"But ye are washed, but ye are sanctified, but ye are justified in the name of the Lord Jesus, and by the Spirit of our God" (I Corinthians 6:11).

"For by one Spirit are we all baptized into one body" (I Corinthians 12:13).

"Ye were sealed with that holy Spirit of promise,

which is the earnest of our inheritance until the redemption of the purchased possession" (Ephesians 1:13-14).

"According to his mercy he saved us, by the washing of regeneration, and renewing of the Holy Ghost" (Titus 3:5).

"And hereby we know that he abideth in us, by the Spirit which he hath given us" (I John 3:24).

Isaiah 28:11-12
* John 3:1-8
  John 7:37-39
  John 14:26
  John 16:13
  John 20:22
* Acts 1:4-8
* Acts 2:1-4
  Acts 2:16-17
  Acts 2:33
* Acts 2:37-39
* Acts 3:19
* Acts 8:15-17
* Acts 9:17
* Acts 10:44-47
* Acts 11:15-18
* Acts 19:1-6
  Romans 5:5

Romans 7:6
* Romans 8:1-16, 23-27
  I Corinthians 2:10-16
  I Corinthians 3:16
  I Corinthians 6:19
* I Corinthians 12:3
  II Corinthians 3:3-18
  Galatians 3:14
  Galatians 4:4-6
  Galatians 5:22-23
  Ephesians 2:18
* Ephesians 3:16-17
  Ephesians 4:30
  II Thessalonians 2:13
  II Timothy 1:7
  I Peter 1:2, 22
  I Peter 4:14
  I John 4:13

4. Speaking in Tongues is the Initial Sign

"And these signs shall follow them that believe . . . they shall speak with new tongues" (Mark 16:17).

"And they were all filled with the Holy Ghost, and began to speak with other tongues, as the Spirit gave them utterance" (Acts 2:4).

"And they of the circumcision which believed were astonished . . . because that on the Gentiles also was poured out the gift of the Holy Ghost. For they heard them speak with tongues" (Acts 10:45-46).

"The Holy Ghost came on them; and they spake with tongues, and prophesied" (Acts 19:6).

---

* Isaiah 28:11-12
  John 3:8
* Acts 2:1-4
  Acts 2:33
* Acts 8:6-8, 12-20
* Acts 10:44-46

* Acts 11:15
  Romans 8:16
  I Corinthians 14:18
* I Corinthians 14:21-22
  James 3:2, 8

III
MIRACLES AND GIFTS
OF THE SPIRIT

"The foundation . . . of laying on of hands"
(Hebrews 6:1-2).

"God also bearing them witness, both with signs and wonders, and with divers miracles, and gifts of the Holy Ghost, according to his own will" (Hebrews 2:4).

A. The Laying on of Hands
1. Symbolic of Transfer; Focuses Faith to Receive

"And he took them up in his arms, put his hands upon them, and blessed them" (Mark 10:16).

"They shall lay hands on the sick, and they shall recover" (Mark 16:18).

"Then laid they their hands on them, and they received the Holy Ghost" (Acts 8:17).

"And when Paul had laid his hands upon them, the

Holy Ghost came on them; and they spake with tongues, and prophesied" (Acts 19:6).

"Paul entered in, and prayed, and laid his hands on him, and healed him" (Acts 28:8).

Genesis 48:14   Mark 6:5
Leviticus 1:4   Mark 7:32
Leviticus 4:4   * Luke 4:40
* Leviticus 16:21   Luke 13:13
Matthew 19:15

2. Consecration or Ordination to Service

"And Joshua the son of Nun was full of the spirit of wisdom; for Moses had laid his hands upon him" (Deuteronomy 34:9).

"When they had prayed, they laid their hands on them" (Acts 6:6).

"And when they had fasted and prayed, and laid their hands on them, they sent them away" (Acts 13:3).

"Neglect not the gift that is in thee, which was given thee by prophecy, with the laying on of the hands of the presbytery" (I Timothy 4:14).

"Stir up the gift of God, which is in thee by the putting on of my hands" (II Timothy 1:6).

Numbers 8:10   * I Timothy 5:22
Numbers 27:18

B. Gifts to the Church

"He gave them power against unclean spirits, to cast them out, and to heal all manner of sickness and all manner of disease. . . . Heal the sick, cleanse the lepers, raise the dead, cast out devils: freely ye have received, freely give" (Matthew 10:1, 8).

"And these signs shall follow them that believe: In my name shall they cast out devils; they shall speak with new tongues; they shall take up serpents; and if they drink any deadly thing, it shall not hurt them; they shall lay hands on the sick, and they shall recover. . . . And they went forth, and preached every where, the Lord working with them, and confirming the word with signs following" (Mark 16:17-18, 20).

"He that believeth on me, the works that I do shall he do also; and greater works than these shall he do" (John 14:12).

"Having then gifts differing according to the grace that is given to us . . . prophecy . . . ministry . . . teaching . . . exhortation . . . he that giveth . . . he that ruleth . . . he that sheweth mercy . . ." (Romans 12:6-8).

"To them that are sanctified in Christ Jesus, called to be saints, with all that in every place call upon the name of Jesus Christ our Lord, both theirs and ours. . . . So that ye come behind in no gift; waiting for the coming of our Lord Jesus Christ" (I Corinthians 1:2, 7).

"For to one is given by the Spirit the word of wisdom; to another the word of knowledge by the same Spirit; to another faith by the same Spirit; to another the gifts of healing by same Spirit; to another the working of miracles; to another prophecy; to another discerning of spirits; to another divers kinds of tongues; to another the interpretation of tongues" (I Corinthians 12:8-10).

"And he gave some, apostles; and some, prophets; and some, evangelists; and some, pastors and teachers" (Ephesians 4:11).

"God also bearing them witness, both with signs and wonders, and with divers miracles, and gifts of the Holy Ghost, according to his own will" (Hebrews 2:4).

——————————

Joel 2:28	Acts 15:32
Luke 10:17-20	Acts 16:16-18
Acts 2:17	Acts 19:6
Acts 4:30	Acts 19:11-12
Acts 5:1-5	Acts 20:9-12
* Acts 5:12-16	Acts 21:9-11
Acts 9:32-42	Acts 27:9-10
Acts 11:27-28	Acts 27:22-25
Acts 14:8-10	Acts 28:1-9

* Romans 12:3-8
  Romans 15:19
  I Corinthians 2:4-5
* I Corinthians 12:1-13
* I Corinthians 12:28-31

I Corinthians 13:1-3, 8-10
* I Corinthians 14:1-40
* Ephesians 4:7-8, 11-16

C. Divine Healing
1. Promise

"I am the LORD that healeth thee" (Exodus 15:26).

"Who healeth all thy diseases" (Psalm 103:3).

"Surely he hath borne our griefs and carried our sorrows . . . and with his stripes we are healed" (Isaiah 53:4-5).

"He cast out the spirits with his word, and healed all that were sick: that it might be fulfilled which was spoken by Esaias the prophet, saying, Himself took our infirmities, and bare our sicknesses" (Matthew 8:16-17).

"And they cast out many devils, and anointed with oil many that were sick, and healed them" (Mark 6:13).

"And these signs shall follow them that believe . . . they shall lay hands on the sick, and they shall recover" (Mark 16:17-18).

"To another the gifts of healing" (I Corinthians 12:9).

"Is any sick among you? let him call for the elders of the church; and let them pray over him, anointing him with oil in the name of the Lord: and the prayer of faith shall save the sick, and the Lord shall raise him up" (James 5:14-15).

Matthew 8:1-15
Matthew 9:1-8, 18-35
* Matthew 10:1, 8
Matthew 12:22
Matthew 14:14, 35-36
Matthew 15:22-31
* Matthew 17:15-21
Matthew 20:30-34
Mark 1:23-42
Mark 2:3-5
Mark 3:1-15
Mark 5:1-43
Mark 6:5-6, 55-56
Mark 7:25-35
Mark 8:22-25
Mark 9:17-27
Mark 10:46-52

Luke 6:18-19
Luke 8:36, 43-56
Luke 9:42
Luke 13:11-13
Luke 17:12-15
Luke 18:35-43
John 4:46-54
Acts 3:1-8, 16
Acts 5:12-16
* Acts 6:8
* Acts 8:6-7, 13
Acts 9:32-43
Acts 14:8-10
* Acts 19:11-12
Acts 28:8-9
* I Peter 2:24

2. Importance of Faith in Jesus

"Thy faith hath made thee whole" (Matthew 9:22; Mark 5:34).

"According to your faith be it unto you" (Matthew 9:29).

56

"Be not afraid, only believe" (Mark 5:36).

"Great is thy faith: be it unto thee even as thou wilt" (Matthew 15:28).

"If thou canst believe, all things are possible to him that believeth. . . . Lord, I believe; help thou mine unbelief" (Mark 9:23-24).

"Go thy way; thy faith hath made thee whole" (Mark 10:52).

"And his name through faith in his name hath made this man strong" (Acts 3:16).

"Paul . . . perceiving that he had faith to be healed, said with a loud voice, Stand upright on thy feet. And he leaped and walked" (Acts 14:9-10).

Matthew 15:28	* Acts 19:13-17
Matthew 17:14-21	* Hebrews 11:6
Mark 2:5	* James 1:6-8
Mark 6:5-6	James 5:14-15

D. Prayers Answered; Needs Supplied

"If I regard iniquity in my heart, the Lord will not hear me: but verily God hath heard me; he hath attended to the voice of my prayer. Blessed be God, which hath not turned away my prayer, nor his mercy from me" (Psalm 66:18-20).

"But seek ye first the kingdom of God, and his righteousness; and all these things shall be added unto you" (Matthew 6:33).

"Ask, and it shall be given you; seek, and ye shall find; knock, and it shall be opened unto you" (Matthew 7:7).

"If ye have faith as a grain of mustard seed, ye shall say unto this mountain, Remove hence to yonder place; and it shall remove; and nothing shall be impossible unto you" (Matthew 17:20).

"And all things, whatsoever ye shall ask in prayer, believing, ye shall receive" (Matthew 21:22).

"If ye shall ask any thing in my name, I will do it" (John 14:14).

"Now to him that is able to do exceeding abundantly above all that we ask or think, according to the power that worketh in us" (Ephesians 3:20).

"I can do all things through Christ which strengtheneth me. . . . But my God shall supply all your need according to his riches in glory by Christ Jesus" (Philippians 4:13, 19).

"Let us therefore come boldly unto the throne of grace, that we may obtain mercy, and find grace to help in time of need" (Hebrews 4:16).

"But let him ask in faith, nothing wavering. For he that wavereth is like a wave of the sea driven with the wind and tossed. For let not that man think that he shall receive any thing of the Lord" (James 1:6-7).

"Ye have not, because ye ask not. Ye ask, and receive not, because ye ask amiss, that ye may consume it upon your lusts" (James 4:2-3).

"Beloved, if our heart condemn us not, then have we confidence toward God. And whatsoever we ask, we receive of him, because we keep his commandments, and do those things that are pleasing in his sight" (I John 3:21-22).

"And this is the confidence that we have in him, that, if we ask any thing according to his will, he heareth us: and if we know that he hear us, whatsoever we ask, we know that we have the petitions that we desired of him" (I John 5:14-15).

Psalm 91:15
Isaiah 55:1-2
Isaiah 65:24
Jeremiah 29:13
* Matthew 7:7-12
Mark 11:24
Luke 11:9
* John 14:12-14
* John 15:7, 16

John 16:23
* Romans 8:26-28
* I Corinthians 10:13
* Philippians 4:6
* Hebrews 4:14-16
* Hebrews 11:6
James 1:5
* James 5:16
I Peter 5:7

IV
HOLINESS AND CHRISTIAN LIVING

"Let us go on unto perfection" (Hebrews 6:1).

"Follow peace with all men, and holiness, without which no man shall see the Lord" (Hebrews 12:14).

A. Principles of Holiness
1. Definition and General Principles

"Present your bodies a living sacrifice, holy, acceptable unto God, which is your reasonable service. And be not conformed to this world: but be ye transformed by the renewing of your mind" (Romans 12:1-2).

"But put ye on the Lord Jesus Christ, and make not provision for the flesh, to fulfil the lusts thereof" (Romans 13:14).

"If any man be in Christ, he is a new creature: old things are passed away; behold, all things are become new" (II Corinthians 5:17).

"Wherefore come out from among them, and be ye separate, saith the Lord, and touch not the unclean thing; and I will receive you. . . . Having therefore these promises, dearly beloved, let us cleanse ourselves from all filthiness of the flesh and spirit, perfecting holiness in the fear of God" (II Corinthians 6:17; 7:1).

"Put off concerning the former conversation the old man, which is corrupt according to the deceitful lusts; and be renewed in the spirit of your mind; and . . . put on the new man, which after God is created in righteousness and true holiness" (Ephesians 4:22-24).

"Work out your own salvation with fear and trembling. For it is God which worketh in you both to will and to do of his good pleasure" (Philippians 2:12-13).

"Abstain from all appearance of evil" (I Thessalonians 5:22).

"But as he which hath called you is holy, so be ye holy in all manner of conversation; because it is written, Be ye holy; for I am holy" (I Peter 1:15-16).

"Be diligent that ye may be found of him in peace, without spot, and blameless. . . . Grow in grace, and in the knowledge of our Lord and Saviour Jesus Christ" (II Peter 3:14, 18).

"My little children, these things write I unto you,

that ye sin not. And if any man sin, we have an advocate with the Father, Jesus Christ the righteous" (I John 2:1).

"Love not the world, neither the things that are in the world. If any man love the world, the love of the Father is not in him. For all that is in the world, the lust of the flesh, and the lust of the eyes, and the pride of life, is not of the Father, but is of the world" (I John 2:15-16).

———————————

Psalm 97:10	Philippians 3:12-16
Matthew 5:48	* I Thessalonians 4:1-8
John 5:14	* Titus 2:11-12
John 8:11	Hebrews 12:1
Romans 6:1-23	* Hebrews 12:14
Romans 14:23	James 1:27
I Corinthians 6:9-11	James 4:4
I Corinthians 9:24-27	James 4:17
* II Corinthians 6:14-7:1	I Peter 2:9
Galatians 4:19	* I John 1:9
* Galatians 5:16-26	* I John 3:4, 8-9
Ephesians 4:13	* I John 3:21-22
Ephesians 5:27	

2. Legalism Versus Faith, Love, and the Spirit

"If ye love me, keep my commandments. . . . If a man love me, he will keep my words" (John 14:15, 23).

"A man is justified by faith without the deeds of the law" (Romans 3:28).

"But now we are delivered from the law, that being dead wherein we were held; that we should serve in newness of spirit, and not in the oldness of the letter" (Romans 7:6).

"For what the law could not do, in that it was weak through the flesh, God sending his own Son in the likeness of sinful flesh, and for sin, condemned sin in the flesh: that the righteousness of the law might be fulfilled in us, who walk not after the flesh, but after the Spirit" (Romans 8:3-4).

"The obedience of faith" (Romans 16:26).

"A man is not justified by the works of the law, but by the faith of Jesus Christ" (Galatians 2:16).

"And hereby we do know that we know him, if we keep his commandments. He that saith, I know him, and keepeth not his commandments, is a liar, and the truth is not in him. But whoso keepeth his word, in him verily is the love of God perfected: hereby know we that we are in him. He that saith he abideth in him ought himself also so to walk, even as he walked" (I John 2:3-6).

---

* Psalm 97:10
* Jeremiah 31:31-33
  Matthew 5:17, 20
* Matthew 22:36-40
* Matthew 23:1-28
  Matthew 28:20

Mark 7:1-23
Luke 18:10-14
Acts 15:1-29
* Romans 1:5
Romans 2:17-29
* Romans 3:19-28

* Romans 7:1-13
* II Corinthians 3:3-18
  II Corinthians 6:17
* Galatians 2:16-21
  Galatians 3:21-25
* Ephesians 2:8-10

  Colossians 2:14-23
* II Timothy 2:5
  Titus 3:8
  Hebrews 10:16
  James 2:14-26
* I John 5:1-4

3. Christian Liberty

"Let us not therefore judge one another any more: but judge this rather, that no man put a stumblingblock or an occasion to fall in his brother's way" (Romans 14:13).

"All things are lawful unto me, but all things are not expedient: all things are lawful for me, but I will not be brought under the power of any" (I Corinthians 6:12).

"But meat commendeth us not to God; for neither, if we eat, are we the better; neither, if we eat not, are we the worse. But take heed lest by any means this liberty of yours become a stumblingblock to them that are weak. . . . But when ye sin so against the brethren, and wound their weak conscience, ye sin against Christ. Wherefore, if meat make my brother to offend, I will eat no flesh while the world standeth, lest I make my brother to offend" (I Corinthians 8:8-9, 12-13).

"All things are lawful for me, but all things edify not. . . . Whether therefore ye eat, or drink, or whatsoever ye do, do all to the glory of God" (I Corinthians 10:23, 31).

"Ye have been called unto liberty; only use not liberty for an occasion to the flesh, but by love serve one another" (Galatians 5:13).

Mark 7:15
John 8:34-36
Romans 3:28
* Romans 6:1-7, 14-15
* Romans 7:5-6
* Romans 8:1-4
Romans 9:31-10:4
* Romans 14:1-6
* I Corinthians 8:8-13
* I Corinthians 10:31-33
Galatians 3:13, 24-25
Galatians 4:1-11, 21-31

* Galatians 5:13-23
* Colossians 2:13-17
* Colossians 3:17
I Thessalonians 5:12-13
I Timothy 5:17
II Timothy 4:2
Hebrews 13:17
James 1:21-25
James 2:8, 12
II Peter 2:18-19
* Jude 4

B. Holiness of Spirit
1. Spiritual Fruit

"But that on the good ground are they, which in an honest and good heart, having heard the word, keep it, and bring forth fruit with patience" (Luke 8:15).

"I am the true vine, and my Father is the husbandman. Every branch in me that beareth not fruit he taketh away: and every branch that beareth fruit, he purgeth it, that it may bring forth more fruit. . . . He that abideth in me, and I in him, the same bringeth forth much fruit: for without me ye can do nothing. . . . I have chosen you, and ordained you, that ye should go and bring forth fruit, and that your fruit should remain" (John 15:1-2, 5, 16).

"For the kingdom of God is . . . righteousness, and peace, and joy, in the Holy Ghost" (Romans 14:17).

"The fruit of the Spirit is love, joy, peace, long-suffering, gentleness, goodness, faith, meekness, temperance" (Galatians 5:22-23).

"For the fruit of the Spirit is in all goodness and righteousness and truth" (Ephesians 5:9).

"Giving all diligence, add to your faith virtue; and to virtue knowledge; and to knowledge temperance; and to temperance patience; and to patience godliness; and to godliness brotherly kindness; and to brotherly kindness charity. For if these things be in you, and abound, they make you that ye shall neither be barren nor unfruitful in the knowledge of our Lord Jesus Christ" (II Peter 1:5-8).

Psalm 16:11
Psalm 18:35
Psalm 126:5
Isaiah 12:3-4
Isaiah 26:3
Nehemiah 8:10
Habakkuk 3:17-18
Matthew 5:5, 9
Luke 10:20

Luke 13:6-9
Luke 21:19
John 14:27
* John 15:1-17
* Romans 1:17
Romans 5:3-5
* Romans 11:22
Romans 12:9-10, 18
* I Corinthians 9:24-27

* I Corinthians 13:1-13	Hebrews 12:1, 14
II Corinthians 10:1	James 1:2-4, 21
* Ephesians 4:1-3	James 3:13
* Philippians 4:4-7	James 4:7-10
* II Timothy 2:24	I Peter 1:8
* Titus 3:2	I Peter 2:21-24
Hebrews 6:12	I Peter 3:4
Hebrews 10:36	* II Peter 1:5-10
Hebrews 11:6	

2. Love

"Love your enemies, bless them that curse you, do good to them that hate you, and pray for them which despitefully use you, and persecute you" (Matthew 5:44).

"Thou shalt love the Lord thy God with all thy heart, and with all thy soul, and with all thy mind. This is the first and great commandment. And the second is like unto it, Thou shalt love thy neighbour as thyself. On these two commandments hang all the law and the prophets" (Matthew 22:37-40).

"A new commandment I give unto you, That ye love one another; as I have loved you, that ye also love one another. By this shall all men know that ye are my disciples, if ye have love one to another" (John 13:34-35).

"Though I speak with the tongues of men and of angels, and have not charity, I am become as sounding brass, or a tinkling cymbal. And though I have the gift of prophecy, and understand all mysteries, and all knowledge; and though I have all faith, so that I could remove mountains, and have not charity, I am nothing. And though I bestow all my goods to feed the poor, and though I give my body to be burned, and have not charity, it profiteth me nothing. Charity suffereth long, and is kind; charity envieth not; charity vaunteth not itself, is not puffed up, doth not behave itself unseemly, seeketh not her own, is not easily provoked, thinketh no evil; rejoiceth not in iniquity, but rejoiceth in the truth; beareth all things, believeth all things, hopeth all things, endureth all things. Charity never faileth. . . . And now abideth faith, hope, charity, these three; but the greatest of these is charity" (I Corinthians 13:1-8, 13).

"But whoso hath this world's good, and seeth his brother have need, and shutteth up his bowels of compassion from him, how dwelleth the love of God in him? My little children, let us not love in word, neither in tongue; but in deed and in truth" (I John 3:17-18).

"If a man say, I love God, and hateth his brother, he is a liar: for he that loveth not his brother whom he hath seen, how can he love God whom he hath not seen?" (I John 4:20).

Leviticus 19:18	* Luke 10:25-37
* Matthew 5:43-48	* John 15:12, 17
Mark 12:28-31	Romans 5:5

Romans 13:8-10   I John 2:7-11
I Corinthians 16:14   * I John 3:10-18, 23
Ephesians 4:1-3, 15   * I John 4:7-21
James 2:8   II John 5
I Peter 1:22

3. Attitudes

"Great peace have they which love thy law: and nothing shall offend them" (Psalm 119:165).

"Pride goeth before destruction, and an haughty spirit before a fall" (Proverbs 16:18).

"Resist not evil: but whosoever shall smite thee on thy right cheek, turn to him the other also" (Matthew 5:39).

"And forgive us our debts, as we forgive our debtors. . . . If ye forgive not men their trespasses, neither will your Father forgive your trespasses" (Matthew 6:12, 15).

"Take heed, and beware of covetousness: for a man's life consisteth not in the abundance of the things which he possesseth" (Luke 12:15).

"God gave them over to a reprobate mind, to do those things which are not convenient; being filled with all unrighteousness, fornication, wickedness, covetousness, maliciousness; full of envy, murder, debate, deceit, malignity; whisperers, backbiters, haters of

God, despiteful, proud, boasters, inventors of evil things, disobedient to parents, without understanding, covenantbreakers, without natural affection, implacable, unmerciful" (Romans 1:28-31).

"Let all bitterness, and wrath, and anger, and clamour, and evil speaking, be put away from you, with all malice: and be ye kind one to another, tenderhearted, forgiving one another, even as God for Christ's sake hath forgiven you" (Ephesians 4:31-32).

"Do all things without murmurings and disputings" (Philippians 2:14).

"For the love of money is the root of all evil" (I Timothy 6:10).

"In the last days perilous times shall come. For men shall be lovers of their own selves, covetous, boasters, proud, blasphemers, disobedient to parents, unthankful, unholy, without natural affection, trucebreakers, false accusers, incontinent, fierce, despisers of those that are good, traitors, heady, highminded, lovers of pleasures more than lovers of God . . . from such turn away" (II Timothy 3:1-5).

"Be swift to hear, slow to speak, slow to wrath: for the wrath of man worketh not the righteousness of God" (James 1:19-20).

"But if ye have respect to persons, ye commit sin" (James 2:9).

"For where envying and strife is, there is confusion and every evil work" (James 3:16).

———————

* Exodus 20:12, 17
* Proverbs 6:16-19
  Proverbs 17:10
  Proverbs 20:3
  Proverbs 29:1
* Matthew 5:21-48
* Matthew 7:1-5
* Matthew 18:21-35
  Mark 11:25-26
* Luke 17:3-5
* Romans 12:9-21
* Galatians 5:19-23
* Ephesians 4:25-32
  Ephesians 5:21

* Philippians 4:11-13
* Colossians 3:5-15
  II Thessalonians 3:11
  I Timothy 5:13, 21
  I Timothy 6:7-19
  Hebrews 12:5, 11
  Hebrews 12:15
* Hebrews 13:17
  James 4:5-6
  I Peter 3:9
  I Peter 4:15
  II Peter 2:10
  I John 3:15

4. Thoughts

"Let the words of my mouth, and the meditation of my heart, be acceptable in thy sight, O LORD" (Psalm 19:14).

"For as he thinketh in his heart, so is he" (Proverbs 23:7).

"For out of the heart proceed evil thoughts . . . these are the things which defile a man" (Matthew 15:19-20).

"Casting down imaginations and every high thing that exalteth itself against the knowledge of God, and bringing into captivity every thought to the obedience of Christ" (II Corinthians 10:5).

"Whatsoever things are true, whatsoever things are honest, whatsoever things are just, whatsoever things are pure, whatsoever things are lovely, whatsoever things are of good report; if there be any virtue, and if there be any praise, think on these things" (Philippians 4:8).

———————

Matthew 5:28   Colossians 2:8
Mark 7:21-23   I John 2:15
I Corinthians 13:5-6

C. The Tongue

"Thou shalt not take the name of the LORD thy God in vain" (Exodus 20:7).

"Whoso privily slandereth his neighbor, him will I cut off" (Psalm 101:5).

"These six things doth the LORD hate: yea, seven are an abomination unto him . . . a false witness that speaketh lies, and he that soweth discord among brethren" (Proverbs 6:16, 19).

"For out of the abundance of the heart the mouth speaketh. . . . Every idle word that men shall speak, they shall give account thereof in the day of judgment. For by thy words thou shalt be justified, and by thy words thou shalt be condemned" (Matthew 12:34, 36-37).

"Bless, and curse not" (Romans 12:14).

"Nor revilers . . . shall inherit the kingdom of God" (I Corinthians 6:10).

"Put off . . . blasphemy, filthy communication out of your mouth. Lie not one to another" (Colossians 3:8-9).

"Speak evil of no man" (Titus 3:2).

"If any man among you seem to be religious, and bridleth not his tongue . . . this man's religion is vain" (James 1:26).

"If any man offend not in word, the same is a perfect man, and able also to bridle the whole body. . . . But the tongue can no man tame; it is an unruly evil, full of deadly poison" (James 3:2, 8).

"Swear not, neither by heaven, neither by the earth, neither by any other oath: but let your yea be yea; and your nay, nay" (James 5:12).

"All liars shall have their part in the lake which burneth with fire and brimstone: which is the second death" (Revelation 21:8).

* Exodus 20:16
Exodus 22:28
Psalm 15:4
Psalm 19:14
Psalm 141:3
Proverbs 11:3
Proverbs 17:9
Proverbs 19:5
Proverbs 26:20-22
* Matthew 5:22, 34-37, 44
* Matthew 12:34-37
Matthew 15:18

Mark 10:19
Romans 1:29-30
I Corinthians 5:11
Ephesians 4:25, 29, 31
* Ephesians 5:4, 12
* Colossians 4:6
Titus 2:8
* James 3:1-12
James 4:11
II Peter 2:10-11
Jude 8-10
Revelation 21:27

D. The Eye

"I made a covenant with mine eyes" (Job 31:1).

"I will walk within my house with a perfect heart. I will set no wicked thing before mine eyes" (Psalm 101:2-3).

"Turn away mine eyes from beholding vanity" (Psalm 119:37).

"He that walketh righteously . . . that stoppeth his ears from hearing of blood, and shutteth his eyes from seeing evil; he shall dwell on high" (Isaiah 33:15-16).

"The light of the body is the eye: therefore when thine eye is single, thy whole body also is full of light;

but when thine eye is evil, thy body also is full of darkness. Take heed therefore that the light which is in thee be not darkness" (Luke 11:34-35).

"Who knowing the judgment of God, that they which commit such things are worthy of death, not only do the same, but have pleasure in them that do them" (Romans 1:32).

"Redeeming the time, because the days are evil" (Ephesians 5:16).

"The lust of the eyes . . . is not of the Father, but is of the world" (I John 2:16).

Genesis 3:6	Matthew 6:22-23
Joshua 7:21	Acts 19:19
II Samuel 11:2	Colossians 4:5
Ecclesiastes 7:29	I Thessalonians 5:22
Matthew 4:8	

E. Adornment and Dress
1. General Principles

"Be not conformed to this world" (Romans 12:2).

"I will therefore that men pray every where, lifting up holy hands, without wrath and doubting. In like manner also, that women adorn themselves in modest apparel, with shamefacedness and sobriety; not with broided hair, or gold, or pearls, or costly array; but (which becometh women professing godliness) with good works" (I Timothy 2:8-10).

"Whose adorning let it not be that outward adorning of plaiting the hair, and of wearing of gold, or of putting on of apparel; but let it be the hidden man of the heart, in that which is not corruptible, even the ornament of a meek and quiet spirit, which is in the sight of God of great price. For after this manner in the old time the holy women also, who trusted in God, adorned themselves" (I Peter 3:3-5).

"The lust of the flesh, and the lust of the eyes, and the pride of life, is not of the Father, but is of the world" (I John 2:16).

---

* Deuteronomy 22:5	II Corinthians 8:21
I Samuel 16:7	Philippians 4:5
Romans 12:17	Philippians 4:11
I Corinthians 9:25	* Titus 2:3-5

2. Immodest Dress

"Behold, there met him a woman with the attire of an harlot, and subtil of heart" (Proverbs 7:10).

"Come down, and sit in the dust, O virgin daughter of Babylon . . . make bare the leg, uncover the thigh, pass over the rivers. Thy nakedness shall be uncovered, yea, thy shame shall be seen" (Isaiah 47:1-3).

"In modest apparel" (I Timothy 2:9).

Genesis 3:7, 21	* Matthew 5:28
Genesis 9:20-25	Luke 8:26-36
Genesis 38:14-19	Acts 19:13-17
Leviticus 18:6-19	* I Peter 3:1-5
II Samuel 11:1-5	

3. Makeup and Hair Dye

"Though thou rentest thy face with painting, in vain shalt thou make thyself fair; thy lovers will despise thee" (Jeremiah 4:30).

"With shamefacedness and sobriety" (I Timothy 2:9).

---

* II Kings 9:30	Proverbs 20:29
Esther 2:13-15	* Ezekiel 23:40
* Proverbs 6:25 (NKJV)	Matthew 5:36
Proverbs 16:31	* I Peter 3:3-4

4. Ornaments and Extravagant Dress

"Though thou deckest thee with ornaments of gold . . . in vain shalt thou make thy self fair; thy lovers will despise thee" (Jeremiah 4:30).

"Not with broided hair, or gold, or pearls, or costly array" (I Timothy 2:9).

"Whose adorning let it not be that outward adorning of plaiting the hair, and of wearing of gold, or of putting on of apparel" (I Peter 3:3).

Genesis 35:1-7
* Exodus 32:2-4
* Exodus 33:4-6
Exodus 35:22
Numbers 31:50-54
Judges 8:24-27
II Kings 9:30

Proverbs 6:16-17
* Isaiah 3:13-23
* Ezekiel 23:26
* Ezekiel 23:40, 42
* Hosea 2:13
Luke 12:33-34
Luke 16:10-13

5. Distinction Between Male and Female

"The woman shall not wear that which pertaineth unto a man, neither shall a man put on a woman's garment: for all that do so are abomination unto the LORD thy God" (Deuteronomy 22:5).

Leviticus 6:10
Leviticus 16:4
Romans 1:26-27

* I Corinthians 6:9-10
* I Corinthians 11:13-15
Revelation 21:27

F. Hair

"Therefore the LORD will smite with a scab the crown of the head of the daughters of Zion. . . . Instead of sweet smell there shall be stink; and instead of a girdle a rent; and instead of well set hair baldness" (Isaiah 3:17, 24).

"Cut off thine hair, O Jerusalem, and cast it away, and take up a lamentation on high places; for the LORD hath rejected and forsaken the generation of his wrath" (Jeremiah 7:29; see 8:5.)

"If it be a shame for a woman to be shorn or shaven, let her be covered. . . . Doth not even nature itself teach you, that, if a man have long hair, it is a shame unto him? But if a woman have long hair, it is a glory to her: for her hair is given her for a covering" (I Corinthians 11:6, 14-15).

"Hair as the hair of women" (Revelation 9:8).

Numbers 6:1-21	Ezekiel 16:7
Deuteronomy 21:10-14	Amos 8:10
Deuteronomy 22:5	Luke 7:37-38
Ezra 9:3	John 11:2
Nehemiah 13:25	John 12:3
Proverbs 16:31	I Corinthians 6:9-10
Isaiah 15:2	* I Corinthians 11:1-16
Jeremiah 47:5	I Timothy 2:9
Jeremiah 48:37	I Peter 3:3
Ezekiel 7:18	

G. Stewardship of the Body

"Wine is a mocker, strong drink is raging: and whosoever is deceived thereby is not wise" (Proverbs 20:1).

80

"Look not thou upon the wine when it is red, when it giveth his colour in the cup, when it moveth itself aright. At the last it biteth like a serpent, and stingeth like an adder" (Proverbs 23:31-32).

"And take heed to yourselves, lest at any time your hearts be overcharged with surfeiting, and drunkenness, and cares of this life" (Luke 21:34).

"Know ye not, that to whom ye yield yourselves servants to obey, his servants ye are to whom ye obey?" (Romans 6:16).

"Know ye not that ye are the temple of God, and that the Spirit of God dwelleth in you? If any man defile the temple of God, him shall God destroy; for the temple of God is holy, which temple ye are" (I Corinthians 3:16-17).

"Nor drunkards . . . shall inherit the kingdom of God" (I Corinthians 6:10).

"All things are lawful for me, but I will not be brought under the power of any" (I Corinthians 6:12).

"What? know ye not that your body is the temple of the Holy Ghost which is in you, which ye have of God, and ye are not your own? For ye are bought with a price: therefore glorify God in your body, and in your spirit, which are God's" (I Corinthians 6:19-20).

"And every man that striveth for the mastery is

temperate in all things. . . . I keep under my body, and bring it into subjection" (I Corinthians 9:25, 27).

"Whether therefore ye eat, or drink, or whatsoever ye do, do all to the glory of God" (I Corinthians 10:31).

Genesis 9:4, 20-25
Genesis 19:32-38
Leviticus 10:8-10
Leviticus 17:10-14
Numbers 6:3
* Numbers 11:32-34
Deuteronomy 21:20
Judges 13:7
* Proverbs 16:32
Proverbs 21:17
Proverbs 23:20-21, 29-35
Proverbs 25:16, 28
Proverbs 31:4-5
* Isaiah 5:11
* Isaiah 28:7
Ezekiel 44:21

* Hosea 4:11
* Habakkuk 2:15
Luke 1:15
* Acts 15:20, 29; 21:25
* Romans 6:12-13
* Romans 12:1
Romans 13:13
* Romans 14:21
II Corinthians 7:1
Galatians 5:19-21
Ephesians 5:18
I Thessalonians 5:22-23
I Timothy 3:3, 8
Titus 1:7
Titus 2:3
I Peter 4:3

H. The Sanctity of Marriage
1. The Marriage Relationship

"Therefore shall a man leave his father and his mother, and shall cleave unto his wife: and they shall be one flesh" (Genesis 2:24).

"To avoid fornication, let every man have his own wife, and let every woman have her own husband. Let the husband render unto the wife due benevolence: and likewise also the wife unto the husband. The wife hath not power of her own body, but the husband: and likewise also the husband hath not power of his own body, but the wife. Defraud ye not one the other, except it be with consent for a time, that ye may give yourselves to fasting and prayer; and come together again, that Satan tempt you not for your incontinency" (I Corinthians 7:2-5).

"The head of every man is Christ; and the head of the woman is the man. . . . Nevertheless neither is the man without the woman, neither the woman without the man, in the Lord" (I Corinthians 11:3, 11).

"Submitting yourselves one to another in the fear of God. Wives, submit yourselves unto you own husbands, as unto the Lord. . . . Husbands, love your wives, even as Christ also loved the church, and gave himself for it. . . . So ought men to love their wives as their own bodies. He that loveth his wife loveth himself" (Ephesians 5:21-22, 25, 28).

"Wives, submit yourselves to unto your own husbands, as it is fit in the Lord. Husbands, love your wives, and be not bitter against them" (Colossians 3:18-19).

"But if any provide not for his own, and specially for those of his own house, he hath denied the faith, and is worse than an infidel. . . . I will therefore that the younger women marry, bear children, guide the house" (I Timothy 5:8, 14).

"Teach the young women to be sober, to love their husbands, to love their children, to be discreet, chaste, keepers at home, good, obedient to their own husbands" (Titus 2:4-5).

"Marriage is honourable in all, and the bed undefiled: but whoremongers and adulterers God will judge" (Hebrews 13:4).

"Husbands, dwell with them according to knowledge, giving honour unto the wife, as unto the weaker vessel, and as being heirs together of the grace of life; that your prayers be not hindered" (I Peter 3:7).

---

* Genesis 2:15-24	Romans 12:10
Leviticus 18:19; 20:18	I Corinthians 6:16, 18
Proverbs 5:15-19	* I Corinthians 7:1-9
Proverbs 31:10-31	* I Corinthians 11:8-12
Song of Solomon 4:9-12	* Galatians 3:28
Song of Solomon 7:1-13	Ephesians 4:2
	* Ephesians 5:21-33
Ezekiel 18:6; 22:10	I Timothy 4:1-3
Acts 5:29	* I Peter 3:1-7

2. Divorce and Remarriage

"Let none deal treacherously against the wife of his youth. For the LORD . . . saith that he hateth putting away" (Malachi 2:15-16).

"That whosoever shall put away his wife, saving for the cause of fornication, causeth her to commit adultery: and whosoever shall marry her that is divorced committeth adultery" (Matthew 5:32; see 19:9).

"Moses because of the hardness of your hearts suffered you to put away your wives: but from the beginning it was not so" (Matthew 19:8).

"What therefore God hath joined together, let not man put asunder. . . . Whosoever shall put away his wife, and marry another, committeth adultery against her. And if a woman shall put away her husband, and be married to another, she committeth adultery" (Mark 10:9, 11-12).

"Whosoever putteth away his wife, and marrieth another, committeth adultery: and whosoever marrieth her that is put away from her husband committeth adultery" (Luke 16:18).

"Let not the wife depart from her husband: But and if she depart, let her remain unmarried, or be reconciled to her husband: and let not the husband put away his wife. . . . The wife is bound by the law as long as her husband liveth; but if her husband be dead, she is at liberty to be married to whom she will; only in the Lord" (I Corinthians 7:10-11, 39).

---

* Genesis 2:23-24
* Leviticus 21:7
  Deuteronomy 24:1-4
  Hosea 2:1-3:3
* Malachi 2:13-16
* Matthew 5:32
  Matthew 18:21-22
* Matthew 19:3-12
* Mark 10:2-12

Luke 17:3-4
John 4:17-18
* Romans 7:1-3
* I Corinthians 7:10-17
  I Corinthians 7:27
  I Timothy 3:1-12
  Titus 1:6
  I Peter 5:3

3. Sexual Immorality

"Thou shalt not commit adultery. . . . Thou shalt not covet thy neighbour's wife" (Exodus 20:14, 17).

"Thou shalt not lie with mankind, as with womankind: it is abomination" (Leviticus 18:22).

"Whosoever looketh on a woman to lust after her hath committed adultery with her already in his heart" (Matthew 5:28).

"Mortify therefore your members which are upon the earth; fornication, uncleanness, inordinate affection, evil concupiscence, and covetousness, which is idolatry" (Colossians 3:5).

"Neither fornicators, . . . nor adulterers, nor ef-

86

feminate, nor abusers of themselves with mankind . . .
shall inherit the kingdom of God. . . . Flee fornication"
(I Corinthians 6:9-10, 18).

Genesis 19:4-11   Mark 7:21-23
Exodus 22:16-19   * Acts 15:20, 29
* Leviticus 18:1-30   * Romans 1:24-27
* Leviticus 20:10-21   I Corinthians 5:1-11
Deuteronomy 5:18   * I Corinthians 6:9-18
Deuteronomy 17:17   II Corinthians 12:21
* Deuteronomy 22:20-30   Ephesians 4:19
Deuteronomy 23:17-18   Ephesians 5:3
Deuteronomy 27:21   * I Thessalonians 4:3-7
Judges 19:22-30   I Timothy 1:10
I Kings 15:12   I Timothy 1:19
I Kings 22:46   II Timothy 2:22
II Kings 23:7   Hebrews 13:4
Joel 3:3   II Peter 2:10
Matthew 15:19-20   Jude 7

4. Marriage with Unbelievers

"If any brother hath a wife that believeth not, and
she be pleased to dwell with him, let him not put her
away. And the woman which hath an husband that
believeth not, and if he be pleased to dwell with her,
let her not leave him" (I Corinthians 7:12-13).

"If her husband be dead, she is at liberty to be married to whom she will; only in the Lord" (I Corinthians
7:39).

"Be ye not unequally yoked together with unbelievers" (II Corinthians 6:14).

Genesis 26:34-35
* Deuteronomy 7:3-4
Numbers 25:1-3
Numbers 31:16
Judges 14:2-3
Judges 16:4-5

I Kings 11:4-8
Ezra 10:1-17
Nehemiah 13:23-31
* I Corinthians 7:10-16
* I Peter 3:1-6

I. The Sanctity of Human Life
1. Violence, Bearing Arms and Killing

"Fear ye not, stand still, and see the salvation of
the LORD. . . . The LORD shall fight for you, and ye
shall hold your peace" (Exodus 14:13-14).

"Thou shalt not kill" (Exodus 20:13).

"But God said unto me, Thou shalt not build an
house for my name, because thou hast been a man of
war, and hast shed blood" (I Chronicles 28:3).

"The angel of the LORD encampeth round about
them that fear him, and delivereth them" (Psalm 34:7).

"But I say unto you, That ye resist not evil: but
whosoever shall smite thee on thy right cheek, turn to
him the other also. . . . Love your enemies, bless them
that curse you, do good to them that hate you, and pray
for them which despitefully use you, and persecute
you" (Matthew 5:39, 44).

"Put up again thy sword into his place: for all they that take the sword shall perish with the sword" (Matthew 26:52).

"And the soldiers likewise demanded of him, saying, And what shall we do? And he said unto them, Do violence to no man" (Luke 3:14).

"For though we walk in the flesh, we do not war after the flesh: (For the weapons of our warfare are not carnal)" (II Corinthians 10:3-4).

"For we wrestle not against flesh and blood" (Ephesians 6:12).

"Ye have condemned and killed the just; and he doth not resist you" (James 5:6).

---

* Genesis 9:5-6	John 17:14, 16
Deuteronomy 5:17	John 18:36
II Kings 6:13-23	Acts 7:60
II Kings 7:6-7	Acts 15:20, 29
II Kings 19:35	Romans 12:17-19
II Chronicles 20:20-25	Galatians 5:19-21
Job 1:9-12	James 2:11
Job 2:6	I Peter 2:18-21
Psalm 91:11	I Peter 3:9
* Matthew 5:38-48	I Peter 4:15
Matthew 15:18-20	I John 3:14-15
John 8:1-11	Revelation 13:10

2. Abortion

"Whoso sheddeth man's blood, by man shall his blood be shed: for in the image of God made he man" (Genesis 9:6).

"If men strive, and hurt a woman with child, so that her fruit depart from her, and yet no mischief follow: he shall be surely punished. . . . And if any mischief follow, then thou shalt give life for life" (Exodus 21:22-23).

"Did not he that made me in the womb make him? and did not one fashion us in the womb?" (Job 31:15).

"Thou hast covered me in my mother's womb. . . . My substance was not hid from thee, when I was made in secret, and curiously wrought in the lowest parts of the earth. Thine eyes did see my substance, yet being unperfect; and in thy book all my members were written, which in continuance were fashioned, when as yet there was none of them" (Psalm 139:13, 15-16).

"Before I formed thee in the belly I knew thee; and before thou camest forth out of the womb I sanctified thee, and I ordained thee a prophet unto the nations" (Jeremiah 1:5).

---

* Job 10:8-12	Matthew 1:18, 20
Psalm 22:10	* Luke 1:15, 41, 44
* Psalm 51:5	* Luke 1:35
Isaiah 49:1-5	I Timothy 2:15

J. Fellowship and Church Judgment

"If thou bring thy gift to the altar, and there rememberest that thy brother hath ought against thee; leave there thy gift before the altar, and go thy way; first be reconciled to thy brother, and then come and offer thy gift" (Matthew 5:23-24).

"If thy brother shall trespass against thee, go and tell him his fault between thee and him alone: if he shall hear thee, thou hast gained thy brother. But if he will not hear thee, then take with thee one or two more, that in the mouth of two or three witnesses every word may be established. And if he shall neglect to hear them, tell it unto the church: but if he neglect to hear the church, let him be unto thee as an heathen man and a publican" (Matthew 18:15-17).

"I have written unto you not to keep company, if any man that is called a brother be a fornicator, or covetous, or an idolater, or a railer, or a drunkard, or an extortioner; with such an one no not to eat" (I Corinthians 5:11).

"Dare any of you, having a matter against another, go to law before the unjust, and not before the saints? . . . Now therefore there is utterly a fault among you, because ye go to law one with another" (I Corinthians 6:1, 7).

"Be ye not unequally yoked together with unbelievers: for what fellowship hath righteousness with unrighteousness?'' (II Corinthians 6:14).

"Now we command you, brethren, in the name of our Lord Jesus Christ, that ye withdraw yourselves from every brother that walketh disorderly, and not after the tradition which he received of us" (II Thessalonians 3:6).

Proverbs 22:24-25   * I Corinthians 6:1-8
* Matthew 18:15-18   I Corinthians 15:33
Luke 5:30-32   * Ephesians 5:11
Acts 2:42   * II Thessalonians 3:6-15
Romans 16:17-18   * I Timothy 6:3-5
* I Corinthians 5:9-11   * II John 9-11

K. Worldly Amusements

"And that which fell among thorns are they, which, when they have heard, go forth, and are choked with cares and riches and pleasures of this life and bring no fruit to perfection" (Luke 8:14).

"And have no fellowship with the unfruitful works of darkness. . . . Redeeming the time, because the days are evil" (Ephesians 5:11, 16).

"Abstain from all appearance of evil" (I Thessalonians 5:22).

"Thou therefore endure hardness, as a good soldier of Jesus Christ. No man that warreth entangleth himself with the affairs of this life" (II Timothy 2:3-4).

"Men shall be lovers of their own selves . . . lovers of pleasures more than lovers of God . . . from such turn away" (II Timothy 3:2, 4-5).

"For we ourselves also were sometimes foolish, disobedient, deceived, serving divers lusts and pleasures" (Titus 3:3).

---

* Deuteronomy 18:9-12
  Isaiah 47:10-15
* Jeremiah 10:2-3
  Psalm 1:1
* Psalm 26:4-5
  Matthew 24:37-39
  Luke 16:10-12
  Acts 16:16-18
  Acts 19:18-20
  Romans 6:16
  Romans 12:2
  Romans 12:17

  Romans 13:13
  I Corinthians 6:12
  I Corinthians 10:23-24
  II Corinthians 8:21
  Galatians 5:19-21
  Colossians 4:5
  II Thessalonians 3:10-12
  Hebrews 11:24-26
  James 4:4
  I Peter 4:3, 7-10
* I John 2:15-16

L. Worship, Emotions, and Music

"Sing unto him a new song; play skilfully with a loud noise" (Psalm 33:3).

"O clap your hands, all ye people; shout unto God with the voice of triumph" (Psalm 47:1).

"Make a joyful noise unto the LORD, all ye lands. Serve the LORD with gladness: come before his presence with singing. . . . Enter into his gates with thanksgiving, and into his courts with praise: be thankful unto him, and bless his name" (Psalm 100:1-2, 4).

"I will praise the LORD with my whole heart, in the assembly of the upright, and in the congregation" (Psalm 111:1).

"Praise ye the LORD. Praise God in his sanctuary: praise him in the firmament of his power. Praise him for his mighty acts: praise him according to his excellent greatness. Praise him with the sound of the trumpet: praise him with the psaltery and harp. Praise him with the timbrel and dance: praise him with stringed instruments and organs. Praise him upon the loud cymbals: praise him upon the high sounding cymbals. Let everything that hath breath praise the LORD. Praise ye the LORD" (Psalm 150:2-6).

"God is a Spirit: and they that worship him must worship him in spirit and in truth" (John 4:24).

"They lifted up their voice to God with one accord. . . . And when they had prayed, the place was shaken where they were assembled together; and they were all filled with the Holy Ghost" (Acts 4:24, 31).

"How is it then, brethren? when ye come together, every one of you hath a psalm, hath a doctrine, hath a tongue, hath a revelation, hath an interpretation. Let all things be done unto edifying. . . . For God is not the author of confusion, but of peace, as in all churches of the saints. . . . Let all things be done decently and in order" (I Corinthians 14:26, 33, 40).

"Where the Spirit of the Lord is, there is liberty" (II Corinthians 3:17).

"Speaking to yourselves in psalms and hymns and spiritual songs, singing and making melody in your heart to the Lord" (Ephesians 5:19).

"Quench not the Spirit" (I Thessalonians 5:19).

"I will therefore that men pray every where, lifting up holy hands" (I Timothy 2:8).

I Samuel 16:23

II Samuel 6:14-16

I Kings 8:22, 54

II Kings 3:15

I Chronicles 6:31-32

* I Chronicles 15:16-29

I Chronicles 23:5

I Chronicles 25:3, 7

* **II Chronicles 5:13-14**

II Chronicles 20:21-22

Nehemiah 8:6-9

Nehemiah 9:3-5

* Psalm 29:2

* Psalm 141:2

* Psalm 149:3-5

Matthew 22:37

Matthew 26:30

Mark 12:30

Luke 7:37-47

* Luke 18:13

* Luke 22:62

Acts 2:13

Acts 3:8

* Acts 4:24-31

Acts 16:25

Romans 8:26

* I Corinthians 14:15, 28

* Colossians 3:16

* Hebrews 13:15

James 5:13

Revelation 1:17

M. Personal Devotion

"Thy word have I hid in mine heart, that I might not sin against thee. . . . I will delight myself in thy statutes: I will not forget thy word. . . . Thy word is a lamp unto my feet, and a light unto my path" (Psalm 119:11, 16, 105).

"When thou doest alms. . . . When ye pray. . . . When ye fast . . ." (Matthew 6:3, 7, 16).

"Examine yourselves, whether ye be in the faith; prove your own selves" (II Corinthians 13:5).

"Praying always with all prayer and supplication in the Spirit, and watching thereunto with all perseverance and supplication for all saints" (Ephesians 6:18).

"Rejoice evermore. Pray without ceasing. In every thing give thanks. . . . Quench not the Spirit. Despise not prophesyings. Prove all things; hold fast that which is good" (I Thessalonians 5:16-21).

"Study to shew thyself approved unto God, a workman that needeth not to be ashamed, rightly dividing the word of truth" (II Timothy 2:15).

"Not forsaking the assembling of ourselves together, as the manner of some is; but exhorting one another: and so much the more, as ye see the day approaching" (Hebrews 10:25).

"Obey them that have the rule over you, and submit yourselves: for they watch for your souls, as they that must give account, that they may do it with joy, and not with grief: for that is unprofitable for you" (Hebrews 13:17).

Psalm 1:1-2
* Psalm 122:1
Matthew 4:4
* Matthew 6:1-18
Matthew 9:14-15
Ephesians 3:16
* Ephesians 4:11-16
Colossians 4:2

I Thessalonians 5:12-13
I Timothy 4:12
I Timothy 5:17
James 1:21
James 5:16
I John 4:1
* Jude 20-21

N. Financial Stewardship
1. Tithes and Offerings

"And he [Abram] gave him tithes of all" (Genesis 14:20).

"Honor the LORD with thy substance, and with the firstfruits of all thine increase" (Proverbs 3:9).

"Will a man rob God? Yet ye have robbed me. But ye say, Wherein have we robbed thee? In tithes and offerings. . . . Bring ye all the tithes into the storehouse, that there may be meat in mine house, and prove me now herewith, saith the LORD of hosts, if I will not open you the windows of heaven, and pour you out a blessing, that there shall not be room enough to receive it" (Malachi 3:8, 10).

"Give, and it shall be given unto you; good measure, pressed down, and shaken together, and running over, shall men give into your bosom. For with the same measure that ye mete withal it shall be measured to you again" (Luke 6:38).

"Even so hath the Lord ordained that they which preach the gospel should live of the gospel" (I Corinthians 9:14).

"He which soweth sparingly shall reap also sparingly; and he which soweth bountifully shall reap also bountifully. Every man according as he purposeth in his heart, so let him give; not grudgingly, or of necessity: for God loveth a cheerful giver" (II Corinthians 9:6-7).

Genesis 28:22	Matthew 23:23
Exodus 36:6	Luke 11:42
Leviticus 27:30	* Luke 16:10-12
Numbers 18:21	Romans 12:8
Deuteronomy 14:22	* I Corinthians 9:7-14
Nehemiah 10:38	II Corinthians 8:7-15
* Malachi 3:8-12	* I Timothy 5:17-18
* Matthew 6:1-4	

2. Integrity in Finances

"Thou shalt not steal. . . . Thou shalt not covet" (Exodus 20:15, 17).

"If thou lend money to any of my people that is poor by thee, thou shalt not be to him as an usurer, neither shalt thou lay upon him usury" (Exodus 22:25).

"He that despiseth the gain of oppressions, that shaketh his hands from holding of bribes . . . he shall dwell on high" (Isaiah 33:15-16).

"Give to him that asketh thee, and from him that would borrow of thee turn not thou away" (Matthew 5:42).

"If therefore ye have not been faithful in the unrighteous mammon, who will commit to your trust the true riches? And if ye have not been faithful in that which is another man's, who shall give you that which is your own?" (Luke 16:11-12).

"Provide things honest in the sight of all men" (Romans 12:17).

"Render therefore to all their dues: tribute to whom tribute is due; custom to whom custom. . . . Owe no man any thing" (Romans 13:7-8).

"Nay, ye do wrong, and defraud, and that your brethren. . . . Nor extortioners shall inherit the kingdom of God" (I Corinthians 6:8, 10).

"Let him that stole steal no more: but rather let him labour, working with his hands the thing which is good, that he may have to give to him that needeth" (Ephesians 4:28).

"If any would not work, neither should he eat" (II Thessalonians 3:10).

"For we brought nothing into this world, and it is certain we can carry nothing out. And having food and raiment let us be therewith content. But they that will be rich fall into temptation and a snare, and into many foolish and hurtful lusts, which drown men in destruction and perdition. For the love of money is the root of all evil: which while some coveted after, they have erred from the faith, and pierced themselves through with many sorrows" (I Timothy 6:7-10).

Exodus 23:8	* Matthew 5:40-42
Leviticus 19:13	Matthew 19:23-26
Deuteronomy 16:18-19	Matthew 22:17-21
Deuteronomy 23:19-20	Matthew 25:27
Psalm 15:5	* Mark 10:19
Psalm 26:10	* Luke 12:13-34
Proverbs 6:1-5	* Luke 16:8-13
* Proverbs 11:15	Luke 19:23
Proverbs 17:23	* II Corinthians 8:21
* Proverbs 28:8	I Thessalonians 4:6
Ezekiel 18:8-17	* I Timothy 5:8
Ezekiel 22:12	* I Timothy 6:5-11

V
RESURRECTION, JUDGMENT AND ETERNITY

"The foundation . . . of resurrection of the dead, and of eternal judgment" (Hebrews 6:1-2).

A. The Second Coming of Jesus Christ

"For many shall come in my name, saying, I am Christ; and shall deceive many. And ye shall hear of wars and rumours of wars: see that ye be not troubled: for all these things must come to pass, but the end is not yet. For nation shall rise against nation, and kingdom against kingdom: and there shall be famines, and pestilences, and earthquakes, in divers places. All these are the beginning of sorrows. Then shall they deliver you up to be afflicted, and shall kill you: and ye shall be hated of all nations for my name's sake. And then shall many be offended, and shall betray one another, and shall hate one another. And many false prophets shall rise, and shall deceive many. And because iniquity shall abound, the love of many shall wax cold. But he that shall endure unto the end, the same shall be saved. And this gospel of the kingdom shall be preached in all the world for a witness unto all nations; and then shall the end come. . . . For there shall arise false Christs, and false prophets, and shall shew great signs and wonders; insomuch that, if it were possible, they shall deceive the elect. . . . For as the lightning cometh out of the east, and shineth even unto the west; so shall also the coming of the Son of man be" (Matthew 24:5-14, 24, 27).

"And there shall be signs in the sun, and in the moon, and in the stars; and upon the earth distress of nations, with perplexity; the sea and the waves roaring; men's hearts failing them for fear, and for looking after those things which are coming on the earth: for the powers of heaven shall be shaken. And then shall they see the Son of man coming in a cloud with power and great glory. And when these things begin to come to pass, then look up, and lift up your heads; for your redemption draweth nigh" (Luke 21:25-28).

"This same Jesus, which is taken up from you into heaven, shall so come in like manner as ye have seen him go into heaven" (Acts 1:11).

"Now we beseech you, brethren, by the coming of our Lord Jesus Christ, and by our gathering together unto him, that ye be not soon shaken in mind . . . as that the day of Christ is at hand. Let no man deceive you by any means: for that day shall not come, except

102

there come a falling away first, and that man of sin be revealed, the son of perdition. . . . For the mystery of iniquity doth already work: only he who now letteth [restrains] will let, until he be taken out of the way" (II Thessalonians 2:1-3, 7).

"Looking for that blessed hope, and the glorious appearing of the great God and our Saviour Jesus Christ" (Titus 2:13).

"Behold, he cometh with clouds; and every eye shall see him, and they also which pierced him: and all kindreds of the earth shall wail because of him. Even so, Amen" (Revelation 1:7).

"And I saw heaven opened, and behold a white horse; and he that sat upon him was called Faithful and True. . . . And he was clothed with a vesture dipped in blood: and his name is called The Word of God. And the armies which were in heaven followed him upon white horses, clothed in fine linen, white and clean. . . . And he hath on his vesture and on his thigh a name written, KING OF KINGS, AND LORD OF LORDS" (Revelation 19:11-16).

"He which testifieth these things saith, Surely I come quickly. Amen. Even so, come, Lord Jesus" (Revelation 22:20).

Zechariah 14:1-9
* Matthew 24:1-51
Matthew 25:1-46
Mark 13:1-37
Luke 12:35-40
* Luke 17:20-37
Luke 18:8
* Luke 21:5-36
John 14:1-3

* Acts 1:9-11
I Thessalonians 4:15-18
I Thessalonians 5:1-3
II Thessalonians 1:7-10
* II Thessalonians 2:1-12
II Peter 3:3-14
* II Timothy 4:8
Jude 14
* Revelation 19:11-21

B. The Catching Away and the Resurrections

"Marvel not at this: for the hour is coming, in the which all that are in the graves shall hear his voice, and shall come forth; they that have done good, unto the resurrection of life; and they that have done evil, unto the resurrection of damnation" (John 5:28-29).

"Behold, I shew you a mystery; We shall not all sleep, but we shall all be changed, in a moment, in the twinkling of an eye, at the last trump: for the trumpet shall sound, and the dead shall be raised incorruptible, and we shall be changed. For this corruptible must put on incorruption, and this mortal must put on immortality" (I Corinthians 15:51-53).

"For our conversation is in heaven; from whence also we look for the Saviour, the Lord Jesus Christ: who shall change our vile body, that it may be fashioned like unto his glorious body" (Philippians 3:20-21).

"We which are alive and remain unto the coming of the Lord shall not prevent them which are asleep. For the Lord himself shall descend from heaven with a shout, with the voice of the archangel, and with the trump of God: and the dead in Christ shall rise first: then we which are alive and remain shall be caught up together with them in the clouds, to meet the Lord in the air: and so shall we ever be with the Lord" (I Thessalonians 4:15-17).

"They lived and reigned with Christ a thousand years. But the rest of the dead lived not again until the thousand years were finished. This is the first resurrection. Blessed and holy is he that hath part in the first resurrection: on such the second death hath no power, but they shall be priests of God and of Christ, and shall reign with him a thousand years" (Revelation 20:4-6).

"And the sea gave up the dead which were in it; and death and hell delivered up the dead which were in them: and they were judged every man according to their works" (Revelation 20:13).

Job 14:14	Luke 20:35-38
* Job 19:25-27	John 11:24-25
* Psalm 17:15	I Corinthians 15:12-23
* Daniel 12:2-3	* I Corinthians 15:33-58
Matthew 22:29-32	Philippians 3:10-14
Mark 12:24-27	Colossians 3:4
Luke 14:14	* I John 3:2

C. The Judgments

"When the Son of man shall come in his glory, and all the holy angels with him, then shall he sit upon the throne of his glory: and before him shall be gathered all nations: and he shall separate them one from another, as a shepherd divideth his sheep from the goats: and he shall set the sheep on his right hand, but the goats on the left. Then shall the King say unto them on his right hand, Come, ye blessed of my Father, inherit the kingdom prepared for you from the foundation of the world. . . . Then shall he say also unto them on the left hand, Depart from me, ye cursed, into everlasting fire, prepared for the devil and his angels" (Matthew 25:31-34, 41).

"For other foundation can no man lay than that is laid, which is Jesus Christ. Now if any man build upon this foundation gold, silver, precious stones, wood, hay, stubble; every man's work shall be made manifest: for the day shall declare it, because it shall be revealed by fire; and the fire shall try every man's work of what sort it is. If any man's work abide which he hath built thereupon, he shall receive a reward. If any man's work shall be burned, he shall suffer loss: but he himself shall be saved; yet so as by fire" (I Corinthians 3:11-15).

"For we must all appear before the judgment seat of Christ; that every one may receive the things done in his body, according to that he hath done, whether it be good or bad. Knowing therefore the terror of the Lord, we persuade men" (II Corinthians 5:10-11).

"And to you who are troubled rest with us, when the Lord Jesus shall be revealed from heaven with his mighty angels, in flaming fire taking vengeance on them that know not God, and that obey not the gospel of our Lord Jesus Christ; who shall be punished with everlasting destruction from the presence of the Lord, and from the glory of his power" (II Thessalonians 1:7-9).

"It is appointed unto men once to die, but after this the judgment" (Hebrews 9:27).

"And I saw a great white throne, and him that sat on it. . . . And I saw the dead, small and great, stand before God; and the books were opened: and another book was opened, which is the book of life: and the dead were judged out of those things which were written in the books, according to their works. And the sea gave up the dead which were in it; and death and hell delivered up the dead which were in them: and they were judged every man according to their works. And death and hell were cast into the lake of fire. This is the second death. And whosoever was not found written in the book of life was cast into the lake of fire" (Revelation 20:11-15).

Matthew 12:41-42	Acts 24:25
Matthew 25:14-30	Romans 14:10-12
Matthew 25:31-46	II Timothy 4:1
John 5:24-29	II Peter 2:4-9
Acts 10:42	II Peter 3:7
Acts 17:31	Jude 14-15

D. The Eternal State
1. Of the Unrighteous

"So shall it be at the end of the world: the angels shall come forth, and sever the wicked from the just, and shall cast them into the furnace of fire: there shall be wailing and gnashing of teeth" (Matthew 13:49-50).

"And cast ye the unprofitable servant into outer darkness: there shall be weeping and gnashing of teeth. . . . Then shall he say also unto them on the left hand, Depart from me, ye cursed, into everlasting fire, prepared for the devil and his angels. . . . And these shall go away into everlasting punishment" (Matthew 25:30, 41, 46).

"And if thy hand offend thee, cut it off: it is better for thee to enter into life maimed, than having two hands to go into hell, into the fire that never shall be quenched: where their worm dieth not, and the fire is not quenched" (Mark 9:43-44).

"And the smoke of their torment ascendeth up for ever and ever: and they have no rest day nor night, who worship the beast and his image, and whosoever receiveth the mark of his name" (Revelation 14:11).

"And the devil that deceived them was cast into the lake of fire and brimstone, where the beast and the false prophet are, and shall be tormented day and night for ever and ever" (Revelation 20:10).

"And death and hell were cast into the lake of fire. This is the second death. And whosoever was not found written in the book of life was cast into the lake of fire" (Revelation 20:14-15).

"But the fearful, and unbelieving, and the abominable, and murderers, and whoremongers, and sorcerers, and idolaters, and all liars, shall have their part in the lake which burneth with fire and brimstone: which is the second death" (Revelation 21:8).

Isaiah 33:14	Matthew 18:8-9
Isaiah 66:24	* Mark 9:43-49
Matthew 5:22, 29-30	Revelation 14:9-11
Matthew 8:12	Revelation 19:20
Matthew 13:40-50	Revelation 22:15

2. Of the Righteous

"Whosoever believeth in him should not perish, but have eternal life" (John 3:15).

"In my Father's house are many mansions: if it were not so, I would have told you. I go to prepare a place for you. And if I go and prepare a place for you, I will come again, and receive you unto myself; that where I am, there ye may be also" (John 14:2-3).

"For he looked for a city which hath foundations, whose builder and maker is God. . . . But now they desire a better country, that is, an heavenly: wherefore God is not ashamed to be called their God: for he hath prepared for them a city" (Hebrews 11:10, 16).

"And I saw a new heaven and a new earth: for the first heaven and the first earth were passed away; and there was no more sea. And I John saw the holy city, new Jerusalem, coming down from God out of heaven, prepared as a bride adorned for her husband. And I heard a great voice out of heaven saying, Behold, the tabernacle of God is with men, and he will dwell with them, and they shall be his people, and God himself shall be with them, and be their God. And God shall wipe away all tears from their eyes; and there shall be no more death, neither sorrow, nor crying, neither shall there be any more pain: for the former things are passed away" (Revelation 21:1-4).

"And the twelve gates were twelve pearls . . . and the street of the city was pure gold, as it were transparent glass. And I saw no temple therein: for the Lord God Almighty and the Lamb are the temple of it. And the city had no need of the sun, neither of the moon, to shine in it: for the glory of God did lighten it, and the Lamb is the light thereof. And the nations of them which are saved shall walk in the light of it: and the kings of the earth do bring their glory and honour into it. And the gates of it shall not be shut at all by day: for there shall be no night there. . . . And there shall in no wise enter into it any thing that defileth, neither whatsoever worketh abomination, or maketh a lie: but they which are written in the Lamb's book of life'' (Revelation 21:21-27).

"And he shewed me a pure river of water of life, clear as crystal, proceeding out of the throne of God and of the Lamb. In the midst of the street of it, and on either side of the river, was there the tree of life, which bare twelve manner of fruits, and yielded her fruit every month: and the leaves of the tree were for the healing of the nations. And there shall be no more curse: but the throne of God and of the Lamb shall be in it and his servants shall serve him: and they shall see his face; and his name shall be in their foreheads. And there shall be no night there; and they need no candle, neither light of the sun; for the Lord God giveth them light: and they shall reign for ever and ever'' (Revelation 22:1-5).

Matthew 6:20
Matthew 8:11
Matthew 25:21, 34, 46
* Mark 10:28-31
Luke 20:35-36
* John 3:15-17, 36
John 5:24-29

II Corinthians 5:1-5
Colossians 1:5
Revelation 7:9-17
* Revelation 19:1-9
* Revelation 21:1-27
* Revelation 22:1-14